COOKING
THE CZECH WAY

Uniform with this volume

COOKING THE FRENCH WAY
Elizabeth Smart and Agnes Ryan

COOKING THE ITALIAN WAY
Dorothy Daly

COOKING THE GERMAN WAY
Nella Whitfield

COOKING THE AUSTRIAN WAY
Ann Knox

COOKING THE SPANISH WAY
Elsa Behrens

COOKING THE CHINESE WAY
Nina Froud

In preparation:

COOKING THE RUSSIAN WAY
Musia Soper

COOKING
THE CZECH WAY

Joža Břízová

Translated by
Helen Watney

SPRING BOOKS

SPRING BOOKS

SPRING HOUSE · SPRING PLACE · LONDON NW5

© *Books for Pleasure Ltd. 1960*

Contents

Introduction

A n early Czech chronicler tells how Čech, the forefather of the Czechs, led his people from afar until he came to the mountain Říp, in Bohemia, and there he decided to settle because it was a very fertile land and rich in game and fish.

The Czech lands, lying in the heart of Europe, were the crossroads of trade and travel routes. Different dishes slowly began to make their way on to the Czech table, at first merely from neighbouring states (Vienna, in particular, for a certain time had a great influence on Czech cooking) but later from further afield as relations with other countries improved. Today, we no longer know whether fried schnitzel, so popular in Czech cooking, was really copied from Vienna, whether the preparation of juicy beefsteaks was really learned in England, potato crisp in France, borshch in Russia and so on.

The recipes in this book are for dishes made by Czech housewives today. We have chosen those which are typical of Czech cooking and are not common in the menus of other countries. For the same reason we have included more sweet than vegetable dishes because Czech cooking is famed for its many delicious cakes and puddings.

Each chapter has a short introduction describing the typical features of the different groups of foods. The recipes have been worked out to serve four persons. Sometimes, however, a pudding or cake provides more helpings. We have given the exact ingredients and best method of preparation.

We have omitted a few special country dishes which are still sometimes prepared for different occasions, but which are not very practical today and are rapidly being forgotten. In the past Czech food has tended to suffer from an excess of carbohydrates - too many floury and sweet dishes, and from an immoderate use of animal fats. These are now giving way to more valuable foods, with the stress on proteins and vitamins.

We hope you will pick out a number of recipes from this book to add variety to your meals, and we are sure that they will not just remain an exotic addition but will soon become firm favourites. We feel justified in thinking this after the great success which Czech dishes, particularly ham, roast pork with dumplings and sauerkraut, beef with cream sauce etc. had at the World Exhibition in Brussels.

Mothers of the older generation, when passing on their culinary arts to their daughters, never forget to remind them of the Czech proverb, 'The way to a man's heart lies through the stomach!' Although the modern woman may not believe that the preparation of food plays quite such an important role in emotional relationships, we hope that this little book on Czech cooking will gain many friends.

Some Useful Facts
and Figures

COMPARISON OF ENGLISH AND AMERICAN
WEIGHTS AND MEASURES

English weights and measures have been used in most of the recipes in this book. The tables on this and the following pages give their conversions into cups and tablespoons. American cups are standard '½-pint' measuring cups, but the American pint is smaller than the British and their half-pint cups are actually equivalent to two-fifths of a British pint.

Liquid Measure

One pint of liquid may be regarded as equal to two American measuring cups for all practical purposes.

3 teaspoons equal 1 tablespoon.

16 tablespoons equal 1 cup.

Solid Measure

1 lb. Butter or other fat	2 cups
1 lb. Flour	4 cups
1 lb. Granulated or Castor Sugar	2 cups
1 lb. Brown (moist) Sugar	$2\frac{2}{3}$ cups
1 lb. Icing or Confectioner's Sugar	3 cups
1 lb. Syrup or Treacle	1 cup
1 lb. Dried Fruit	2 cups
1 lb. Chopped Meat (finely packed)	2 cups
1 lb. Lentils or Split Peas	2 cups
1 lb. Coffee (unground)	$2\frac{2}{3}$ cups
1 lb. Breadcrumbs	4 cups
$\frac{1}{2}$ oz. Flour	1 level tablespoon
1 oz. Flour	1 heaped tablespoon
1 oz. Syrup or Treacle	1 tablespoon
1 oz. Sugar	1 level tablespoon
1 oz. Jam or Jelly	1 level tablespoon
$\frac{1}{2}$ oz. Butter	1 tablespoon smoothed off

FRENCH MEASURES

It is difficult to convert to French measurements with absolute accuracy, since 1 oz. is equivalent to 28.352 grammes. The table below is therefore very approximate.

Liquid Measure

Approximately $1\frac{3}{4}$ English pints may be regarded as equal to 1 litre.

1 demilitre is half a litre, and 1 decilitre is one-tenth of a litre.

Solid Measure

1 oz. is equal to approximately 30 grammes.
Approximately 2 lb. 3 oz. is equal to 1 kilogramme.

COOKING TEMPERATURES

Water

Simmering 180° F.
Boiling   212° F.

Oven Temperatures

	Electricity °F	Gas Regulo No.
COOL	225—250	0—½
VERY SLOW	250—275	½—1
SLOW	275—300	1—2
VERY MODERATE	300—350	2—3
MODERATE	350—375	4
MODERATELY HOT	375—400	5
HOT	400—450	6—7
VERY HOT	450—500	8—9

Note: This table is an approximate guide only. Different makes of cooker vary and if you are in any doubt about the setting it is as well to refer to the manufacturers' temperature chart.

To convert °F. to °C., subtract 32° and multiply by $\frac{5}{9}$.
To convert °C. to °F., multiply by $\frac{9}{5}$ and add 32°.

Glossary

AU GRATIN — A dish coated with sauce, sprinkled with cheese or crumbs, browned in the oven or under the grill, and served in the dish in which it is cooked.

BAIN-MARIE — A shallow pan of water into which a cooking vessel may be put to enable it to cook more slowly.

BAKING BLIND — Baking a pastry case without a filling. To keep its shape, cover the surface of the uncooked pastry with greased greaseproof paper, greased side down, and fill the shell with haricot beans or dried peas kept for this purpose.

BASTING — Pouring hot fat over meat or poultry at intervals during the cooking to prevent it becoming dry on the outside.

BLANCH — To soak in boiling water for a few minutes or to bring to boil, and then throw the water away.

BOUILLON — A meat broth, not clarified.

BOUQUET GARNI — A mixture of herbs (parsley, thyme, bay leaf etc.) tied loosely in a muslin and used to flavour soups, stews and sauces.

CLARIFIED FAT — Fat heated, skimmed and strained, to be used for greasing tins, etc.

CREAMING — Mixing fat and sugar together with a wooden spoon until the mixture is light and creamy in both colour and texture. It is the process used for many cake and pudding mixtures.

CROUTE — A thick slice of fried bread on which a savoury may be served.

CROUTONS — Very small dice or fancy shapes of fried bread served with soup, etc.

DROPPING CONSISTENCY — The texture of a cake or pudding mixture before it is cooked. To test this, fill a spoon with mixture, which should drop in about 5 seconds, without the spoon being jerked.

FOLDING IN — Combining whisked or creamed mixture with other ingredients to retain lightness — for instance, in making soufflés. Draw a spoon across the bottom of the bowl, take up a spoonful of the mixture and bring it over the dry ingredients on top, thus 'folding' them in. Repeat this process until the two mixtures are combined, but do not beat the mixture as the bubbles in it must not be broken.

GLAZING — Brushing pastry, scones, etc. with beaten egg or milk, usually before baking. A sweet glaze can be made by dissolving 1 teaspoon sugar in 1 teaspoon water. New potatoes or carrots can be tossed in butter to glaze.

JULIENNE — A clear soup containing vegetables cut in matchlike strips.

MACEDOINE — A mixture of cut or small cooked vegetables or mixed fruit served as a salad or dessert.

MARINADE — A mixture of lemon juice or vinegar with seasonings and herbs, in which meat or fish may be soaked before cooking to improve its flavour.

PUREE — A smooth pulp made by sieving meat, fruit or vegetables cooked in liquid.

REDUCING — Boiling a sauce to reduce its quantity and thicken it.

ROUX — Flour and fat cooked together (with or without browning them) as a basis for thickening gravies, soups.

RUBBING IN — A way of mixing fat and flour for cakes and pastry. Cut the fat into small pieces in the flour, then rub it into the flour with the fingertips, lifting the mixture well out of the bowl to incorporate air.

SAUTE — To toss meat or vegetables in a little hot fat in a covered saucepan, to improve their flavour.

SCORING — Cutting across the surface of fish to enable it to be cooked more quickly. The crackling of pork is also scored for easier carving.

SEASONED FLOUR — 1 tablespoon flour mixed with 1 teaspoon salt and $\frac{1}{8}$ teaspoon pepper, used to improve the flavour of meat and fish.

SPONGING — In bread making there are five stages before baking: mixing, sponging, kneading, rising and proving. Sponging, which is often referred to in this book, means mixing the yeast with a little sugar and warm milk, making a well in some flour, pouring in the yeast mixture and leaving it to 'sponge' for a while. In English cookery the yeast mixture is usually poured into the whole of the flour to be used and the 'well' is covered completely with flour. The bowl is then covered with a cloth and left in a warm place until the yeast has bubbled and broken through the top crust of flour. In these Czech recipes you will find that the yeast mixture is left to sponge with only a little flour, and then the rest of the ingredients are added later. Either method is satisfactory. The most important thing to remember when cooking with yeast is to allow enough time for the yeast to sponge (20—30 minutes), to rise (after you have kneaded the dough, 2—3 hours) and to prove (the final stage before baking, when you leave the dough to rise in the tins for 15—20 minutes).

VANILLA SUGAR — Vanilla sugar can be obtained by cutting a vanilla pod into 4 or 5 pieces and keeping in an airtight jar with 2 lb. sugar. The same pod can be used for about 2 months, the jar being refilled with sugar as required.

SOUPS

In Czechoslovakia soup forms the introduction to lunch and sometimes supper. Family menus do not usually include hors d'oeuvre, and the soups are therefore more filling. Factory and farm workers often eat soup in midmorning. Special garnishes for clear poultry and beef soups are served on festive occasions. But even at ordinary meals meat broths are not served without some addition; diced meat and vegetables are left in the broth and such garnishings as noodles, rice, little dumplings, etc. are added.

Thick soups are typical of Czech cooking. Either a light-coloured thickening is used, which makes a white, creamy soup, or a dark roux is added and the soups are brownish in colour. People often add milk, cream, or yeast to soups and there are a number of potato soups which are spiced in an original way - with dill, marjoram, fresh or dried mushrooms. Soups are made filling by adding egg yolk, butter, cream or cheese. Extra nourishment, too, comes from the addition of green garnishes, rich in vitamin C, such as parsley, chives and dill.

There is no doubt about it - Czech soups make a very satisfying beginning to a meal for a hungry family!

FAMILY BEEF SOUP

3 pints water
1 lb. stewing beef, bones
   and liver
4 oz. mixed vegetables
   (carrot, celeriac, cabbage,
   parsley root, onion)

2 oz. rice or vermicelli
1 tablespoon dripping
parsley or chives
salt, pinch of pepper

Wash bones and meat, place in cold salted water, cover and simmer for about 3 hours, adding hot water from time to time to make up for what boils away. Clean and dice vegetables and sauté in fat. When the meat is soft, remove from the water and cut into small pieces. Strain liquid and add meat and vegetables. Boil for a few minutes and then add rice, 'liver rice' (see p. 18, recipe for Liver Dumplings) or vermicelli. Serve garnished with fresh, finely chopped parsley or chives.

BEEF SOUP WITH CABBAGE AND RICE

3 pints water
1 lb. beef
1 large cabbage

2 oz. rice
salt and pepper

Pour boiling water over beef and simmer for about 3 hours. Add only boiling water during cooking so that it does not go off the boil. Then strain soup, cut meat into small pieces and return to pan. Season and add finely shredded cabbage and rice. Boil for about 5 minutes uncovered to allow pungent cabbage smell to escape.

LIVER DUMPLINGS FOR BEEF SOUP

4 oz. calves' or ox liver	about 3 oz. breadcrumbs
1 tablespoon butter	1 garlic clove
1 egg	salt, pinch of pepper

Beat together butter and salt, add egg, finely minced liver, crushed garlic, pinch of pepper and enough breadcrumbs to form small round dumplings. Boil them in beef soup or bouillon for about 5 minutes. If fewer breadcrumbs are added to the liver, the mixture can be pressed through a coarse-grained sieve to give *liver rice*.

OMELETTE NOODLES FOR BEEF SOUP

2 oz. flour	fat for frying
1 gill milk	salt
1 egg	

Beat egg into milk, slowly add flour. Fry thin omelettes in greased pan. Cut omelettes crosswise into thin strips. Add to beef bouillon. The strips can also be fried quickly again to make them crisp.

BATTER PUDDING FOR BEEF BOUILLON

3 egg whites
1 tablespoon butter
3 tablespoons breadcrumbs
1 tablespoon fresh mushrooms

1 tablespoon chopped pars-ley
fat for greasing baking tin
salt

Melt butter and allow to cool, then add to whisked egg whites alternately with breadcrumbs. Finally add chopped mushrooms, which have been simmered for about 10 minutes, and finely chopped parsley. Pour mixture into baking tin, which has been greased with unmelted fat and sprinkled with breadcrumbs, and bake in moderate oven until golden brown. Cut finished pudding into small cubes, place a little on each plate and pour on hot bouillon.

OXTAIL SOUP

3 pints water
1 lb. oxtail
4 oz. root vegetables
2 peppercorns

pinch of allspice
salt
parsley

Wash and clean oxtail, cut into sections and boil in salt water. Add diced vegetables and seasoning and cook for 2—3 hours. Sprinkle finely chopped parsley into soup at last minute and serve either with a section of tail on each plate or remove meat from bones and cut into small pieces. A little coarse semolina, rice or pasta may also be cooked in the soup.

QUICK SOUP FROM MINCED MEAT

3 pints water
8 oz. minced beef
about 4 oz. root vegetables
handful of rice

salt
parsley
1 meat cube or few drops of
    meat extract

Place cleaned and diced vegetables and minced meat in pot, cover with cold water and boil for about 30 minutes. Add salt, meat cube and at last minute, finely chopped parsley. A handful of rice can also be added.

CREAM OF VEAL SOUP WITH PEAS

3 pints water
1 lb. neck of veal
1 cup fresh or frozen green peas
2 oz. plain flour

2 oz. butter
1 bread roll
fat for frying
salt

Simmer veal in salted water until soft. Remove sinews and gristle and cut into small pieces. Add a light roux made from the flour and butter to the liquid, whisk well and boil for a few minutes. Return meat to soup and add peas, again boiling for a few minutes. Serve with fried croûtons made from bread roll.

FRESH PORK SOUP

3 pints water
8 oz. pig's head (fresh from kill)
2 oz. root vegetables
1 oz. groats
handful of dried mushrooms
salt
drop of meat extract

Wash meat and boil in salt water together with vegetables and mushrooms until soft. Take out meat, remove from bone and cut into small pieces. Add groats and meat extract and boil for a few minutes. Serve with a slice of black bread.

THICK GOULASH SOUP

3 pints water
8 oz. beef (shin)
3 large potatoes
3 oz. fat
1½ oz. flour
3 oz. vegetables
1 onion

Seasoning: pinch pepper
½ teaspoon red pepper
¼ teaspoon crushed caraway seeds
meat extract (optional)
salt

Finely chop onion, cut up meat into small pieces and fry gently in part of the fat until nearly soft. Then pour boiling water over meat, add brown roux made from rest of fat and flour, finely sliced vegetables and diced potatoes. Cook for 15 minutes. The soup must have a good spicy taste. To obtain this add salt, a pinch of pepper, ½ teaspoon red pepper, ¼ teaspoon crushed caraway seeds and, if liked, a few drops of meat extract.

SMOKED MEAT SOUP

3 pints stock from ham or
   smoked meat
1 oz. plain flour
1 oz. lard

about 4 oz. root vegetables
2 tablespoons semolina
1 frankfurter
parsley

Make light brown roux from fat removed from stock, lard and flour, pour over stock and whisk well. Add diced vegetables and boil for a short time. Then add semolina, small pieces of frankfurter or chopped smoked meat and finely chopped parsley. Do not salt soup as stock is salty enough.

CREAMY SMOKED MEAT SOUP

3 pints stock from smoked
   meat
1 oz. lard
1 oz. plain flour
1 gill sour cream

2 egg yolks
2 slices bread
a little fat for frying bread
parsley

Make light roux from lard and flour, dilute with stock and cook for about 30 minutes. Then add cream mixed with yolks and warm in soup. Do not reboil. Cut bread into small strips or cubes and quickly fry in fat to make them crisp. Place a little on plates together with finely chopped parsley and pour over hot soup. Do not salt soup—the stock is salty enough.

CHICKEN SOUP

3 pints water
1 small hen (about 2 lb).
4 oz. root vegetables

1½ oz. vermicelli
salt

Clean hen and cook in salted water together with diced vegetables for about 2 hours. Remove hen which can then be eaten with red pepper sauce. Return heart, liver, gizzard, wings and neck, from which bones have been removed, and finely chopped vegetables. Add home-made vermicelli and chopped chives or parsley. If the soup is to be the main dish, serve a quarter of the hen to each person and eat with bread and rolls.

CLEAR GIBLET SOUP

3 pints water
giblets from goose or duck
 (gizzard, heart, neck,
 wings, feet and a bit of
 liver)
1 tablespoon parsley

4 oz. vegetables (carrot, celeriac, green peas, parsley root, onion)
salt
pinch mace

Clean giblets, i.e. singe off hairs, blanch and peel feet, pull skin off gizzard etc. Place in cold water with salt and mace and simmer for 2—3 hours until soft. Remove meat from bones and cut into small pieces. Put cleaned, diced vegetables and meat into stock and boil for about 10 minutes. Vermicelli or rice may be added. At last minute add finely chopped parsley.

CREAMY GIBLET SOUP

3 pints water	1 egg yolk
giblets from goose or duck	1 cup cream
2 oz. butter	salt
2 oz. plain flour	pinch of mace
3 oz. root vegetables	1 tablespoon parsley

Simmer cleaned giblets in water for about 2 hours, until soft. Strain off stock and add water to make up to 3 pints again. Prepare light roux from butter and flour, whisk into stock and boil for a few minutes. Add cleaned, diced vegetables and meat, which has been removed from bones and cut into small pieces, and boil for about 10 minutes. Add salt and a pinch of mace and before serving whisk in cream and yolk and add finely chopped parsley.

CREAMY BRAIN SOUP

3 pints water	½ onion
1 brain (veal)	1 egg yolk
2 oz. butter	3 oz. root vegetables
2 oz. flour	parsley
	salt

Boil cleaned and diced vegetables in water, thicken with light roux made from butter and flour, and cook for about 30 minutes. Lightly fry blanched and skinned brain in butter together with chopped onion. Add to sieved soup and season with salt, beaten yolk and spoonful of chopped parsley.

CHRISTMAS FISH SOUP

3 pints water
1 head, 2 tails and innards
of carp
4 oz. root vegetables
2 oz. flour

2 oz. butter
fat for frying bread for
croûtons
parsley
salt
few drops of meat extract

Remove eyes and gills from head and simmer head in water together with tails. Cook liver, milt and roes separately. When soft, remove bones and cut flesh into small pieces. Make a light roux with butter and flour, pour on strained stock and boil for about 20 minutes. Then add finely chopped vegetables, flesh and innards and cook for another 10 minutes. Add salt, a few drops of extract and finely chopped parsley. Serve with fried croûtons.

POTATO SOUP

3 pints water
3 oz. fat
4 large potatoes
½ onion
1 small carrot
1 small parsley root
2 oz. flour

¼ celeriac
3 oz. fresh mushrooms or 1 tablespoon dried mushrooms
1 garlic clove
salt
pinch marjoram

Cut up mushrooms, dice root vegetables and boil together in water. From fat and flour make light roux, add to soup, whisk well and boil for 15 minutes. Add diced potatoes, crushed garlic and finally marjoram and boil. The soup is thick.

SIEVED POTATO SOUP

2 pints water
6 medium-sized potatoes
1 pint milk
1 teaspoon butter

1 egg yolk
salt, parsley
Garnish: 1 oz. flour
1 egg

First prepare the garnish. Work egg with flour and a little water to a stiff, elastic dough, grate onto a clean towel and leave to dry. Boil potatoes in water, pass through sieve and add milk. Add salt to taste and throw in garnish. Boil about 5 minutes. Before serving whisk in fresh yolk, and add butter and parsley. Do not boil again.

SOUP FROM SPRING HERBS

3 pints water
2 handfuls chopped herbs
   (tansy, ground ivy, strawberry leaves,
   nettle)
2 oz. fat
2 oz. plain flour

1 egg yolk
1 bread roll
fat for frying
salt

Make light roux from fat and flour and pour over water or stock, whisk well and boil for 15 minutes. Add chopped green leaves, allow to come to boil and then break in fresh yolk. Serve with fried croûtons. This soup is usually served early in spring, around Easter.

LEEK SOUP

3 pints water
8 oz. leeks
3 oz. fat
2 oz. plain flour
1 egg yolk

1 gill milk
3 potatoes
1 bread roll
fat for frying
salt

Cut the well-washed white part of the leeks into rings and fry some of the fat. From the rest of the fat and the plain flour prepare a light roux, pour over water, and add peeled, cut potatoes, the green part of the leeks and salt and boil for a few minutes. Then pass soup through sieve and at last minute add fresh yolk and a few fried rings of leek. Serve with fried croûtons made from bread roll.

CAULIFLOWER SOUP WITH BREAD DUMPLINGS

3 pints water
1 cauliflower
2 oz. fat
2 oz. flour
salt, pinch of mace

Dumplings: 1 egg
3 oz. breadcrumbs
1 teaspoon butter
little milk
parsley

Boil cauliflower in salt water. When nearly soft remove from pot, thicken liquid with light roux made from fat and flour, add mace and cook for 20 minutes. Then boil dumplings in soup and finally add cauliflower fleurettes.
To make dumplings, first moisten breadcrumbs with milk. Cream butter, egg and salt, add breadcrumbs and parsley. Form dough into tiny dumplings and cook in soup for 3—5 minutes.

SAUERKRAUT SOUP

2½ pints water   1 oz. butter
8 oz. sauerkraut   1 oz. flour
8 oz. potatoes   1 egg yolk
½ pint sour cream   salt, caraway seeds, vinegar

Chop sauerkraut into small pieces, peel and dice potatoes. Boil with a few caraway seeds in salt water. Then whisk flour with cream, add to soup and allow to come to boil. Before serving add a fresh yolk and a knob of butter. Add vinegar to taste.

CELERIAC AND LEMON SOUP

3 pints water   1 egg yolk
1 small celeriac   juice from ½ lemon
2 oz. plain flour   1 bread roll
3 oz. butter   fat for frying
1 tablespoon milk   salt

Cut celeriac into small pieces and boil in salt water until soft. Make a light roux from flour and fat, add stock and sieved celeriac and boil for about 20 minutes. Before serving add egg, whisked in milk, and finally lemon juice. Serve with fried bread cut into thin strips.

CREAMY GARLIC SOUP

3 pints water   1 oz. butter
4 large potatoes   1 egg yolk
1 gill milk   salt
4 garlic cloves   meat extract (optional)

Crush peeled garlic with salt. Peel and dice potatoes and boil
in water. Add salt, butter, yolk and meat extract. Place
crushed garlic on plates and pour on hot soup.

TOMATO PUREE SOUP

3 pints water   1 oz. plain flour
2 oz. tomato purée   ½ onion
2 tablespoons rice   lemon
    or pasta   salt, pinch of sugar
2 oz. fat

Fry onion in fat, add flour and a little water to make a light
roux. Add tomato purée and water and cook for about 20
minutes. Season with salt, sugar and lemon juice to taste.
2 tablespoons of rice or pasta may be added and the soup
boiled for a few minutes.

OATMEAL SOUP

3 pints water or stock
4 tablespoons oatmeal
2 tablespoons root vegetables

2 tablespoons grated cheese
salt
pinch of mace
1 cup milk (optional)

Clean vegetables and cut into pieces. Cover oatmeal and vegetables with water and boil for about 30 minutes. Pass through a sieve and dilute with water to bring up to 3 pints again. Add salt and a pinch of mace. Serve with grated cheese. A cup of milk may be added to this soup.

PULSE SOUP WITH FRANKFURTER

3 pints water
3 oz. dried peas or lentils
1 frankfurter
1 oz. fat
1 oz. flour

$\frac{1}{2}$ onion
1 garlic clove
pinch of sweet red pepper
salt

Soak pulse overnight in unsalted water. Next day cook in the same water until soft enough to pass through a hair-sieve. Make a light roux from the fat and flour, pour over the purée, stir well and cook for 15 minutes. Then add grated onion, crushed garlic, salt and a pinch of red pepper. Before serving chop in small rounds of frankfurter or pieces of smoked sausage.

CREAMY MUSHROOM SOUP (KULAJDA)

2 pints sour cream	8 oz. fresh mushrooms
1 pint water	1 tablespoon dill
4 large potatoes	a few caraway seeds
2—3 eggs	vinegar
2 oz. plain flour	salt

Clean and cut up the mushrooms and simmer in water with caraway seeds. After about 30 minutes add flour, mixed with cream, and diced raw potatoes. Cook for about 15 minutes. Before serving add 2—3 well-beaten eggs, salt, a few drops of vinegar and chopped dill.

FARM CARAWAY SEED SOUP

3 pints water	1 teaspoon caraway seeds
2½ oz. plain flour	1 teaspoon meat extract
1½ oz. noodles	salt
2 oz. butter or lard	

Make a light roux from the fat and flour, pour over cold water, whisk well and cook for a few minutes. Then add caraway seeds, salt, meat extract (optional) and noodles or pasta.

YEAST SOUP

3 pints water	small pieces of carrot, celeriac, parsley
3 oz. baker's yeast	root and onion
2 oz. plain flour	parsley
2 oz. butter	salt

Pasta: 1 egg, 3 tablespoons milk, about 3 oz. fine semolina

Fry onion and yeast in butter. When yeast begins to brown at edges, sprinkle on flour, mix and pour on water. Add finely chopped vegetables, season with salt, whisk well and cook for 20 minutes. Now prepare pasta. Beat egg in a little milk, add a little flour at a time and salt. Using a teaspoon drop small pieces of dough into soup and cook for about 5 minutes. This soup is rich in vitamin B2.

QUICK SOUP FROM EGG ROUX

3 pints water	1 tablespoon plain flour
2 eggs	chopped parsley
1 oz. fat	salt
3 tablespoon grated root vege-	meat extract (optional)
tables	

Melt fat, add flour and make light roux. Add 2 beaten eggs and stir until the mixture curdles. Pour on cold water and beat well. Add grated vegetables, salt and cook for about 15 minutes. A teaspoon of meat extract may be added (optional) and finely chopped parsley.

SEMOLINA SOUP

3 pints water   1 meat cube
2 oz. semolina   chopped parsley
1 tablespoon butter

Melt fat in pan, allow semolina to brown slightly in it and then pour on cold water. Add a meat cube, beat well and simmer for a few minutes. Before serving add chopped parsley.

CHEESE SOUP

2½ pints water   1 oz. butter
½ pint sour cream   chopped parsley
3 potatoes   salt
3 oz. grated Parmesan cheese

Peel potatoes and cook in salted water. Pass through sieve and add grated cheese. Simmer for a few minutes, then add cream and fresh butter. Before serving add chopped parsley.

SOUR MILK SOUP

2 pints water   1 oz. butter
1 pint sour milk or cream   caraway seeds
4 eggs   salt
1 oz. flour

Make a light roux from flour and butter, dilute with cold water, whisk well and cook for about 20 minutes. Mix in sour cream or milk and break in one egg after another. Break eggs just above surface and allow to slip into boiling soup, carefully using fork to cover yolk with white, so that they remain whole. Serve with hot potatoes which have been boiled in their jackets and then peeled.

COLD SOUP

3 pints water   4 tablespoons butter
4 apples   ½ lemon
3 heaped tablespoons flour   a little sugar

Wash apples but do not peel, cut up into small pieces and cook in water. Make a light roux from the butter and flour, add to apples, mix well and cook for 15 minutes. Pass soup through sieve, add a pinch of sugar, a little lemon peel and juice and allow to cool. Serve with sponge fingers or biscuits.

Czechoslovakia, whose national anthem states that it looks like an earthly paradise, is a land rich in fertile fields, deep forests and plenteous rivers and lakes. A well-developed animal husbandry supplies the market with good quality beef and excellent pork from fine Czech pigs, whose hams have made Czechoslovakia famous the world over. It also breeds sheep, kids and lambs, which add variety to menus, particularly in the spring.

Poultry farming supplies the market with fattened geese, turkeys, ducks, hens, cocks and chickens. The Czech housewife not only roasts and fries them but also uses them to prepare many other tasty dishes.

Although Czechoslovakia has no sea, it has many large ponds and rivers rich in fish. Mountain streams provide trout and throughout the year carp are available. Carp is a traditional Christmas dish, like turkey in England.

Apart from rabbits and hares, which are very popular, the winter meals are brightened up with venison and wild boar's meat.

Many changes have taken place in the last ten years in the preparation of meat dishes. Instead of the rich elaborate roasts which required great preparation and are expensive, the Czech housewife who goes out to work is learning to make simpler but equally tasty dishes. Even the simplest dish requires a certain amount of care. Not only a good recipe but also a love of good food and a gourmand's desire for perfection are necessary to obtain crisp roast pork, to make a good thick cream sauce or to delicately season a pâté.

It is important that the protein part of these main course dishes (usually meat) should be supplemented by foods rich in vitamins and mineral salts. For this reason some of the recipes give a suitable combination of meat and vegetables or state what vegetable salad is served with them.

PIQUANT BEEFSTEAK

1 lb. beefsteak (4 steaks)   3 garlic cloves
2 tablespoons oil   salt

Wash the steaks, remove all fat and skin, and beat lightly with
a small mallet or the reverse end of a knife. Pat back into
shape, rub the surface with crushed garlic and salt and fry
quickly on both sides. Serve with fried potatoes or rice.

BEEF IN GINGER SAUCE

2 lb. shoulder of beef   1 onion
2 oz. fat bacon   1 level teaspoon ground ginger
2 oz. dripping   salt
2 slices black bread

Wash the meat, beat with a mallet and lard with strips of
bacon (i.e. draw strips of bacon through the surface of the
meat with a special larding needle, or needle with a very large
eye). Sprinkle with salt and ginger. Fry the finely chopped
onion in the dripping, add the meat and quickly fry all over.
Then add a little water and two slices of dry bread which will
dissolve in the sauce and thus thicken it. Simmer until the
meat is soft. Pass the sauce through a sieve. Serve with
dumplings or boiled rice.

ROAST BEEF AND MUSHROOMS

2 lb. beef (leg, steak)	3 oz. butter
4 oz. fresh mushrooms	1 onion
2 oz. bacon	caraway seeds
1 tablespoon plain flour	salt

Wipe a good fillet of beef, season with salt and lard with strips of bacon. Fry onion in butter, add meat and fry lightly on all sides. Add a little water and simmer until tender. Cook mushrooms and a few caraway seeds separately in a teaspoon of fat. Dredge the meat with flour, allow to brown slightly, add a little water and boil for a few minutes. Pass sauce through sieve and then add the mushrooms. Cut the meat into slices and pour mushroom sauce over them. Serve with dumplings, rice or potatoes.

BEEF ROULADE

2 lb. beef (leg)	1 tablespoon French mustard
1 lb. minced pork	1 onion
2 oz. dripping or lard	salt

Buy a flat piece of topside, wipe and beat well with a mallet. Season with salt and smear with French mustard and minced pork, mixed with chopped onion. Roll and tie up. Fry quickly in fat and then put in oven and roast until tender, basting from time to time. Cut the meat crosswise into slices and serve with dumplings or potatoes.

ZNOJMO GOULASH

2 lb. beef (shin)
2 oz. dripping or lard
1 tablespoon plain flour
1 onion

2 pickled cucumbers
pinch pepper
salt

Wipe meat, cut into small pieces and season with salt and pepper. Fry the finely chopped onion in the fat, add the meat and fry quickly. Then add a little water and simmer until tender. When the liquid evaporates, sprinkle on the flour, allow to brown slightly, then add a little water and cook well. Add the diced cucumbers to the sauce and serve with dumplings or potatoes. Chopped tomatoes and paprikas may be added instead of the cucumbers.

STEAKS IN CAPER SAUCE

1 lb. steak (4 steaks)
2 oz. bacon
1 oz. lard or dripping
1 tablespoon flour
1 gill sour cream

2 tablespoons capers
2 tablespoons French mustard
1 onion
salt and pepper

Wipe the steaks, remove all fat, nick the sides to prevent them curling and beat lightly with a mallet. Season with salt and pepper and sprinkle with flour. Fry quickly on both sides on chopped onion. Add mustard, capers and a little water, cover and simmer till tender. Take the meat out of the sauce and allow the latter to brown, then add cream mixed with the flour and boil. Return steaks to sauce and serve with dumplings or potatoes.

BEEF ROLLS

1 lb. beef (4 slices from leg)	1 onion
4 thin slices bacon (3 oz.)	French mustard
2 oz. dripping	pepper
1 tablespoon plain flour	salt
2 pickled cucumbers	celeriac, carrot (optional)

Wipe the slices of meat, season with salt and pepper and
lightly spread with mustard. On each slice place a thin piece
of bacon, chopped cucumber and onion. Finely chopped
celeriac and a small piece of carrot may also be added.
Carefully roll up each piece and secure with thread or a small
skewer. First fry each roll on all sides and then add a little
water and simmer until tender. Remove rolls, allow juice to
evaporate and sprinkle a little flour on the fat. Add a little
water or stock, stir well and boil for a few minutes. Serve
with rice, potatoes or macaroni.

BEEF WITH CREAM SAUCE

1 fillet of beef (about 2 lb)
7 oz. root vegetables (carrot,
    parsley root, celeriac)
½ pint sour cream
1 tablespoon flour
2 oz. bacon

2 oz. dripping or lard
1 onion
vinegar, lemon, salt
Seasoning: 5 peppercorns
      pinch allspice
      ½ bayleaf

Wash fillet, clean well and remove fat and gristle. Thread strips of bacon through surface of meat. Lightly fry onion, chopped vegetables and seasoning in baking tin, add meat and cook in moderate oven until brown, adding a little water from time to time. Then take out meat and cut into slices. Add sour cream, mixed with flour, to sauce and simmer for a few minutes. Pass finished sauce through sieve, together with vegetables, so that it is brownish and thick. Add salt, a few drops of vinegar or a piece of lemon peel and juice, according to taste. Serve with dumplings.

TARTAR BEEFSTEAK

1 lb. fillet of beef
1 egg yolk
1 onion
1 garlic clove

a little Worcester sauce
salt
½ teaspoon French mustard
Seasoning: pepper, sweet red pepper,
      caraway seeds

Wipe the meat and remove all fat and membrane. Mince finely or break up in an emulsifier. Place on a plate, make a dent in the middle and break a fresh egg yolk into it. Garnish the meat with thin rings of onion, ground pepper, red pepper, garlic crushed with salt, mustard and caraway seeds. Tartar beefsteak is served raw and each guest adds whatever garnish he prefers, then spreads the beefsteak on black bread.

FRIED BEEF CAKES

1 lb. minced beef	8 slices black bread
2 oz. fat	1 onion
2 tablespoons plain flour	salt, pepper, French mustard

Whisk the finely minced beef with the water and flour. Season with salt and pepper and leave for 1 hour. Then, using wet hands, form the mixture into small flat cakes, fry quickly in hot fat. Place the cakes on slices of black bread smeared with mustard and decorate with chopped raw onion.

RISSOLES

1 lb. minced meat (beef and pork)	1 tablespoon flour
	breadcrumbs (about 2 oz.)
½ onion	4 oz. fat for frying
2 oz. bacon	salt
2 eggs	

Fry finely chopped bacon and onion in pan until onion is golden brown. When cold add to minced meat together with 1 egg, a few breadcrumbs and salt, and form rissoles. Dip each rissole into flour, egg and breadcrumbs and fry in fat. Serve with mashed or boiled potatoes.

ROAST MINCED MEAT

1 lb. beef	bread
8 oz. pork	1 onion
2 oz. bacon	fat for frying
2 eggs	salt and pepper
3 bread rolls (about 4 oz.)	

Wipe beef and pork and mince finely. Chop onion and fry in a little fat until golden brown. Cut bacon into cubes and heat slightly until it has a glassy effect. Put meat, onion and bacon into bowl, add beaten eggs, rolls which have been soaked in water, salt, pepper and enough breadcrumbs to form a firm roll. To prevent the roll burning at the bottom it may be placed on a grid. Smooth the surface with wet hands or wipe with egg white. Cook in moderate oven for about 1 hour adding a little water from time to time. Cut into slices and serve with potatoes and salad or compote.

MEAT PUDDING

1 lb. meat	breadcrumbs
3 eggs	1 teaspoon brandy
2 oz. bacon	ground pepper
2 oz. butter	lemon rind
1 gill milk	salt

Any kind of minced meat can be used (beef, veal, poultry, or cooked meat). Add the egg yolks, chopped bacon, salt, pepper and brandy and a little grated lemon rind (optional). If the mixture is too stiff add a little milk, if too soft add a few breadcrumbs. Finally fold in stiffly beaten whites. Turn into a greased and breadcrumbed pudding bowl and steam for about 1 hour. Turn out and cut into slices. Serve with hot vegetables or potatoes and a vegetable salad.

OX TONGUE WITH ANCHOVIES

1 small ox tongue (8 oz.)	1 teaspoon breadcrumbs
2 oz. bacon	a little anchovy paste
3 oz. butter	1 onion
	salt

Wipe the tongue and cook in salted water till tender. Then skin it and cut into slices. Beat a little over half the butter with the anchovy paste and smear on each slice of tongue. Sprinkle with a few fine breadcrumbs, dot with butter and place in a greased fireproof dish or baking tin. Bake in a moderate oven until the surface turns slightly brown. Serve with potatoes.

STUFFED BREAST OF VEAL

2—3 lb. breast of veal	*Stuffing:* 3 bread rolls (about 5 oz.)
3—4 oz. butter	1 tablespoon butter
	2—3 egg yolks
	1 gill milk
	3—4 egg whites
	parsley, salt

Wipe meat, cut bones and carefully make a cavity to take the stuffing. Cut the rolls into small pieces, place in a bowl and cover with warm milk in which the salt, 1 tablespoon butter and the egg yolks have been mixed. When the milk has been absorbed mix in the finely chopped parsley and stiffly beaten whites. Fill the cavity and sew up. Melt the butter in a large baking tin or casserole, place the meat on it with the stuffed side upwards and cook in a moderate oven, adding a little hot water from time to time. When the meat is slightly brown on the top, turn it over and brown on the other side. Cut the breast into portions along the bones, taking care that the stuffing does not fall out. Serve with mashed or fried potatoes or with potato salad.

VEAL ROULADE WITH FRANKFURTERS

2 lb. shoulder of veal
2 frankfurters
3 eggs
2 oz. bacon

3 oz. butter
1 pickled cucumber
salt

Cut the veal so that it lies flat. Wipe and beat gently with a mallet until it is quite thin. Sprinkle with salt, spread on scrambled eggs, dot with diced bacon and cucumber and place frankfurters lengthwise. Roll up so that the frankfurters are in the middle and the rest of the filling around them, and secure with thread. Sprinkle with flour and place in the oven with hot fat. Add a little hot water from time to time. When the roulade is brown and soft, cut it crosswise in slices. Serve with rice, boiled or mashed potatoes.

VEAL ROULADE WITH VEGETABLES

2 lb. shoulder or leg of veal
4 oz. butter
1 small carrot, a piece of celeriac and parsley root
1 tablespoon green peas

1 onion
1 pickled cucumber
a little anchovy paste
salt

Parboil the root vegetables in a little salted water. Then dice, add peas and mix with anchovy paste beaten with a small piece of butter. Beat the veal well with a mallet, smear with the vegetable mixture and roll up. Secure well to prevent unrolling during roasting. Place on melted butter and cook in a moderate oven till brown, adding a little water from time to time. Cut the roll into slices, and serve with mashed potatoes or rice.

VEAL STEW WITH DUMPLINGS

2 lb. veal	parsley
2 oz. butter	lemon rind and juice
2 tablespoons plain flour	a pinch of mace
½ onion	salt

a small piece each of carrot, celeriac and parsley root

Dumplings: 2 egg yolks   8 oz. breadcrumbs
            2 oz. butter   salt
            4 tablespoons milk

Clean and cut up the vegetables and onion and fry in the fat. Add the meat, cut into small pieces and seasoned with salt, and simmer until tender. Then dredge with flour, add water and boil for a few minutes. Season this thick sauce with grated lemon rind and juice, mace and finely chopped parsley. Prepare the dumplings in a bowl. First beat the fat, yolks and salt and then add the crumbs soaked in milk. Form into little balls and throw into boiling salted water. Cook for about 5 minutes. Remove from water, allow to cool and then add to meat and sauce. Cooked cauliflower fleurettes may also be added.

VEAL IN RED PEPPER SAUCE

2 lb. veal	1 onion
3 oz. butter	ground red pepper
½ pint sour cream	salt
1 tablespoon plain flour	

Wipe the meat and cut into small pieces. Fry onion in fat, add meat and fry quickly all over. Then sprinkle on red pepper, season with salt and add a little water. Cover and simmer till soft. Whisk flour in cream, add to meat and cook for about 20 minutes. Serve with dumplings or rice.

VEAL MEDALS

2 lb. veal (leg)   1 teaspoon plain flour
3 oz. butter   salt
1 teaspoon oil

Wipe the meat and cut into small rounds, lightly beat with mallet, season with salt and run through skewer or tooth-pick to prevent them curling when cooked. Quickly fry in oil, then transfer them to a casserole containing melted butter and gently cook till tender, adding a little water. When cooked, lightly sprinkle them with flour, add a little water and simmer for a few minutes. Serve with peas and potatoes, giving each person 2 to 3 pieces of meat.

VEAL ROLLS

4 slices veal   1 gill sour cream
2 oz. bacon   parsley
1 oz. fat   lemon rind
1 tablespoon flour salt

Wipe meat, beat lightly with mallet and season with salt. Finely chop the bacon, parsley and lemon rind and place on slices of meat. Roll up and secure with thread or skewer. Dip rolls in flour and quickly fry in fat, add a little water and simmer. When tender, pour cream mixed with flour over meat and allow to boil for a few minutes. Serve with potatoes or dumplings.

VEAL SCHNITZEL IN BATTER

4 slices veal   1 oz. grated cheese
2 eggs   parsley
2 tablespoons plain flour   salt
4 oz. fat for frying

Wipe the slices of meat and beat lightly with a mallet. To prepare the batter mix the beaten eggs with the flour, salt, finely chopped parsley and grated cheese. Dip the meat in the batter and quickly fry on both sides in hot fat. Serve with potatoes and vegetables or with potato salad.

VEAL SCHNITZEL AU NATUREL

4 slices veal   1 lemon
3 oz. fat   salt
1 teaspoon plain flour

Lightly beat the meat with a mallet, season with salt and quickly fry in fat on both sides. Then sprinkle the meat with flour, allow to brown slightly and add a little water. Cook well. Add a pinch of finely grated lemon rind and a few drops of lemon juice to the sauce. Serve with potatoes, rice or macaroni.

BRNO SCHNITZEL

4 slices veal	1 tablespoon plain flour
2 oz. ham	1 tablespoon milk
1 egg	1 teaspoon fine breadcrumbs
1 green peas	salt
2 oz. butter	4 oz. fat for frying

Clean the meat, beat lightly with a mallet and season with salt. Scramble the egg in a pan together with the butter, green peas and chopped ham. Spread a little of the mixture on each slice of veal, fold the meat in half and secure with a small skewer. Then carefully dip the meat in flour, egg and breadcrumbs and fry in hot fat.

MINCED VEAL SCHNITZEL

1 lb. veal	pinch of mace
3 oz. butter	1 tablespoon parsley
1 tablespoon plain flour	salt

Make a roux from a tablespoon of butter and the flour, dilute with 2 tablespoons water and boil for a few minutes. The sauce should be very thick. Add the minced meat, season with salt, parsley and mace. With wet hands form the mixture into small flat cakes and fry quickly on both sides in butter.

SHELLED DEVILS

1 lb. veal	1 teaspoon breadcrumbs
1 calf's brain (5 oz.)	1 cup grated cheese
3 eggs	1 cup green peas
3 oz. butter	1 lemon
1 teaspoon plain flour	salt
1 onion	

Fry the finely chopped veal and onion very slowly in part of the fat till the meat is soft. Sprinkle with the flour, then pour on a little water and cook for a few minutes. Blanch the brain, fry gently in a little fat and add to the sauce. Season the mixture with salt, a little grated lemon rind and juice and add the eggs and cooked green peas. Grease some shells, or small fireproof dishes, and sprinkle with breadcrumbs. Place a little of the mixture on each, sprinkle with grated cheese and dot with fresh butter. Cook in a hot oven for about 10 minutes. Serve with a slice of lemon and white bread.

VEAL RISOTTO

1 lb. veal	2 tablespoons plain flour
1 lb. rice	2 tablespoons grated Parmesan
3 oz. butter	1 lemon
3 egg yolks	salt
1 cup green peas	

Cut up the meat into small pieces and stew in a little butter till tender. When soft, sprinkle with flour, add a little water and the peas and cook for a few minutes. Season the sauce with salt, a pinch of lemon peel and a few drops of lemon juice. Fry the rice separately in the rest of the fat, pour on 1½ pints boiling salted water and simmer till soft. Mix the rice with the meat and sauce. Place a small mound on each plate and sprinkle with grated cheese.

FRIED CALVES' OR PIGS' LIVER

4 slices liver (1 lb.)   1 teaspoon plain flour
2 oz. bacon   1 onion
2 tablespoons oil   salt
1 teaspoons butter

Wash the liver and cut into slices. Thread pieces of bacon through and fry quickly in hot oil for about 3 minutes on both sides. Season with salt, place on a plate and sprinkle with a few onion rings. Heat the oil left in the pan, sprinkle with flour, allow to brown, then add a little water and simmer for a few minutes. Finally add a knob of fresh butter to the sauce. Pour the sauce over the liver and serve with rice or boiled potatoes.

BRAIN WITH EGGS

2 calves' or pigs' brains   1 onion
    (about 6 oz.)   parsley
4 eggs   salt
1 tablespoon butter

Blanch the brain. Fry the chopped onion in fat until a golden brown, add the brain and cook gently for about 10 minutes. Then add the beaten eggs, season with salt and stir until the eggs curdle. Serve with chopped parsley sprinkled on top.

STEWED KNUCKLE OF VEAL

2 knuckles of veal (about
    2 lb.)
3 oz. butter
1 teaspoon plain flour

3 peppercorns
pinch allspice
½ bayleaf
salt

Wipe the knuckles, season with salt and fry quickly in the butter. Add a little water and the seasoning, cover and simmer gently until tender. Remove the meat, sprinkle the liquid with flour, add a little more water and cook for a few minutes. Remove the meat from the bones and return to the pan to heat through. Serve with rice, potatoes or macaroni.

PIG'S HEAD WITH HORSERADISH

2 lb. meat from pig's head,
    tongue and heart
piece of horseradish

French mustard
salt

Boil a piece of pig's head, tongue and heart in salt water for about 2 hours until soft. Place on a plate, season well with salt and serve hot with mustard or horseradish. Use the stock for a soup.

ROAST PORK

| 2 lb. pork from neck or loin | 1 teaspoon caraway seeds |
| | salt |

Wipe the meat and if it is very fat nick the skin slightly. Season all over with salt, place on a baking tin and sprinkle with caraway seeds. Add a little water at first to prevent the joint from getting too brown on the surface and too dry. When the fat begins to run, baste well so that it browns gently. Roast pork is traditionally served with dumplings and stewed cabbage. For dumplings see p. 96, for cabbage p. 126.
The meat may also be roasted with a clove of garlic (farm fashion) and then served with cabbage and potato dumplings.

STUFFED BREAST OF PORK

2 lb. fat breast	salt
Stuffing: 2 bread rolls (3 oz.)	1 oz. breadcrumbs
3 eggs	parsley
1 gill milk	salt
1 oz. fat	

Wipe the meat, season with salt and make a cavity in it. Beat the fat with the egg yolks and salt, add diced rolls which have been soaked in milk, the finely chopped parsley and finally the stiffly whisked egg whites. If necessary, add a few bread-crumbs to make it stiffer. Fill the meat with the mixture, sew up and place on a baking tin with the stuffed side upwards. Cook in a moderate oven, adding a little hot water from time to time. The fat soon starts to flow from the meat which should be basted frequently with the fat and water mixture so that it browns well. Serve with boiled potatoes or dumplings and cabbage. Cold roast breast is served with potato salad.

PORK CUTLETS WITH CARAWAY SEEDS

1 lb. pork (4 cutlets)   caraway seeds
1 tablespoon plain flour   salt
1 oz. lard or dripping

Wipe the cutlets, beat gently with a mallet, cut the edges to prevent curling, season with salt and fry quickly in dripping. Then add a little water and a few caraway seeds and stew till tender. When soft dredge with flour, add salt and a cup of water and cook for a few minutes. Serve with dumplings.

CUTLETS WITH TOMATOES

Prepare in the same way as for cutlets with caraway seeds but add a few sliced tomatoes and paprikas (optional) when stewing.

CUTLETS WITH FRENCH MUSTARD

Prepare as for cutlets with caraway seeds but add 2 teaspoons of French mustard and some cream before serving.

PORK CUTLETS WITH MUSHROOMS

1 lb. lean pork (4 cutlets) 1 tablespoon plain flour
4 fresh mushrooms (large) caraway seeds
3 oz. butter salt

Fry the chopped mushrooms in part of the butter. Beat the
cutlets and cut at the edges, dust with flour and fry quickly
on both sides. Add the meat to the mushrooms and stew for
a few minutes. When soft, sprinkle with flour, season add
a little water and cook for about 10 minutes. Serve with
dumplings, potatoes or rice.

QUICK PORK CUTLETS

1 lb. (4) pork or veal cutlets *Garnish:* 3 tomatoes
2 tablespoons oil 1 green paprika
½ teaspoon flour
salt

Beat the cutlets with a mallet, season with salt, cut the edges
to prevent curling and fry in oil in an iron pan. Then dredge
the juice with flour and cook for a few minutes. Return
cutlets to sauce, add a few rings of paprika and tomatoes and
stew for a few minutes. Serve with rice or potatoes.

BOILED HAM OR SMOKED PORK

1 small ham or 2 lb. smoked loin

Put the smoked ham into a large pot of boiling water and simmer for about 2 hours so that the meat is cooked through. The meat must leave the bones if pricked with a skewer. Remove the meat from the water, allow to cool slightly and then cut into slices with a sharp knife. The skin must first be removed, working from the broader end towards the bone. Serve the ham hot with pea purée or mashed potatoes. It can also be served cold with French mustard or grated horse-radish.

POTATO SHAKE WITH SMOKED MEAT

2 lb. potatoes	3 oz. lard or dripping
8 oz. salami or smoked meat	salt
7 oz. fine semolina	

Use potatoes boiled the previous day. Grate them finely onto a board and leave for a few minutes to dry. Then sprinkle on the semolina and salt and shake lightly with the hands so that the semolina is evenly distributed but do not knead into a dough. Put half into a well greased baking tin, sprinkle with finely chopped meat and half the melted fat and add rest of potatoes. Sprinkle the surface well with the rest of the fat and bake in a hot oven until brown. Cut into large squares and serve with hot vegetables or raw vegetable salad.

POTATO ROLL WITH SMOKED MEAT

2 lb. potatoes
8 oz. smoked meat
1 lb. fine semolina
1 egg
3 oz. dripping or lard

2 tablespoons breadcrumbs
1 onion
3 oz. butter
salt

Use potatoes boiled the previous day. Grate them onto a board, sprinkle with semolina and salt, add egg and work into a dough. Carefully roll out, sprinkle with fat, fried onion, finely chopped cooked meat and a few fried breadcrumbs. Carefully roll up, place on a wet serviette and tie up the ends. Place the roll in a large pot of boiling water and cook for 45 minutes. Then remove roll from serviette and cut into slices with a sharp knife or wire. Place a few slices on each plate, sprinkle with melted butter and fried onion. Serve with hot spinach or cabbage or with vegetable salad.

MEAT JELLY

2 lb. meat from pig's head
1 calves' foot
a few pieces of pig's skin
1 small carrot
piece of celeriac

parsley root
1 small onion
vinegar or lemon juice
3 peppercorns
salt

Wipe the meat and boil in water together with the vegetables and seasoning. When the vegetables are soft remove them and allow meat to cook until tender. Cut the meat into small pieces and place in a bowl together with the chopped vegetables. Pour over the strained stock, which has been seasoned with salt and vinegar or lemon juice. Allow to cool and set. If a layer of fat rises to the surface, skim it off. It can be used in other dishes. Turn out the jelly and cut into slices. Serve with freshly chopped onion and vinegar or lemon.

PIG'S KIDNEYS

4 kidneys (1 lb.)	2 pinches caraway seeds
3 tablespoons oil	pinch pepper
1 teaspoon plain flour	salt
1 onion	

Cut each kidney lengthwise, remove fat and wash well to remove pungent smell. Then cut it into slices. Heat oil in a large iron frying pan, add kidneys, caraway seeds and pepper (do not salt) and fry quickly for about 8 minutes. Finally add a teaspoon of plain flour, a little water and cook. Season with salt before serving. Serve with rice, potatoes or a salted roll.

MUTTON RIBS WITH MUSTARD

4 mutton ribs	$\frac{1}{2}$ teaspoon plain flour
2 tablespoons oil	ground pepper
1 tablespoon French mustard	salt

Cut the ribs at the edges and fry quickly on both sides in oil. Dredge with a little plain flour, add salt, pepper, mustard and a little water and allow to cook until the meat is tender. Pour the strained sauce over the ribs and serve with rice.

MINCED BEEFSTEAKS WITH TOMATO SAUCE

1 lb. minced mutton	1 onion
1 egg	1 teaspoon flour
1 small tin tomato purée	breadcrumbs
2 oz. bacon	salt
2 oz. fat	

Finely mince the meat and onion, season with salt, mix with the chopped bacon and the egg and thicken with a few breadcrumbs. Form into small flat rounds, fry quickly in fat, then add a little water and simmer for about 20 minutes. Then remove the beefsteaks, sprinkle the juice with flour, add the purée and a little water and cook well. Strain the sauce over the beefsteaks and serve with rice or potatoes.

MUTTON WITH GARLIC

2 lb. saddle of mutton	1 onion
4 oz. dripping or lard	2 cloves of garlic
1 tablespoon flour	salt

Wipe the meat and remove the fat. Rub with garlic crushed with salt, place on onion lightly fried in dripping and cook in moderate oven, adding a little water and basting from time to time. When tender, remove and cut into slices. Allow the juice to evaporate, dredge with flour and let it brown slightly, add a little water and cook for a few minutes, stirring well.

MUTTON IN MARJORAM

2 lb. undercut of mutton   1 onion
2 oz. butter   1 teaspoon marjoram
1 tablespoon plain flour   salt
3 oz. vegetables (carrot, celeriac and parsley root)

Wipe the meat, cut into large pieces and stew in butter together with onion and vegetables. When the meat is nearly soft, allow the juice to evaporate, dredge with plain flour and add a little water. Mix well and cook for a few minutes. When the sauce is nearly ready add the marjoram and season with salt. Serve with potatoes.

STUFFED ROAST KID

1 front portion of kid (4 lb.)   *Stuffing:* 3 egg whites
5 oz. butter   2 egg yolks
1 tablespoon breadcrumbs   1 oz. butter
salt   2 bread rolls (3 oz.)
                                   1 gill milk
                                   parsley
                                   salt

Clean the meat, rinse and wipe with a paper napkin. Carefully make a cavity for the stuffing. Cut the rolls into small pieces and sprinkle with milk. Cream the butter with the yolks and salt, add the moist rolls, finely chopped parsley and finally the stiffly whisked whites. Stuff the cavity and sew up with thread. Place the meat, stuffed side upwards, on melted butter, sprinkle with breadcrumbs, and cook in the oven, basting from time to time. Serve with potatoes or potato salad.

HEN SERVED IN SOUP

1 hen (about 2 lb.)
1 oz. vermicelli
5 oz. root vegetables
    (carrot, celeriac, parsley)

1 tablespoon green peas
$\frac{1}{2}$ teaspoon soup extract
salt

Clean the hen and offal and cook in boiling salt water. After about 30 minutes add the finely chopped vegetables and peas and cook until the hen is tender. Remove the hen and cut into portions. Pull the meat off the wings and cut it and the liver, gizzard and heart into small pieces, returning them to the soup. Boil some vermicelli or rice in the soup and serve with a piece of hen on each plate.

HEN IN RED PEPPER SAUCE

1 hen (about 2 lb.)
3 oz. butter
$\frac{1}{2}$ pint sour cream
2 teaspoons plain flour

1 onion
1 teaspoon sweet red pepper
salt

Clean the hen and singe off the hairs. Fry the chopped onion in butter in a baking tin, add the red pepper and seasoned hen and cook in the oven, adding a little water and basting at intervals. Then cut it into portions, thicken the juice with cream in which the flour has been whisked and cook for a few minutes. Serve with dumplings, macaroni or rice.

FRIED CHICKEN

1 chicken (about 2 lb.)	2 oz. breadcrumbs
1 egg	8 oz. fat (butter) for frying
2 oz. plain flour	salt

Clean a young chicken and cut into quarters. Carefully remove the larger bones, run a skewer through each portion to prevent curling during cooking, season with salt and dip in flour, egg and breadcrumbs. Fry quickly in fat.

ROAST STUFFED CHICKEN

1 chicken (about 2 lb.)	*Stuffing:* 1 tablespoon butter
3 oz. butter	3 egg yolks
salt	2 tablespoons milk
	4 oz. breadcrumbs
	3 egg whites
	chopped parsley

Clean the chicken and singe the hairs, then prepare the breast for stuffing. The stuffing is made as follows: cream the butter, salt and egg yolks, add the breadcrumbs which have been soaked in the milk, the chopped parsley and finally the stiffly whisked whites. Stuff the breast first and sew up. If some stuffing remains, put it inside the bird. Place the chicken on melted butter and roast till tender and golden brown, adding a little water and basting at intervals. Serve with mashed or fried potatoes.

CAPON IN WHITE SAUCE

1 capon (about 2 lb.)	pinch of mace
1 oz. butter	1 lemon
1 oz. plain flour	salt
a few root vegetables	

Clean the capon and simmer with a little water and the vegetables. When nearly tender, divide into into portions, and allow to finish cooking in the white sauce which has been prepared as follows: make a light roux from the butter and flour, dilute with stock, boil for a few minutes, season with salt, lemon peel and juice and a pinch of mace. Serve with potatoes.

ROAST GOOSE OR DUCK

1 goose (about 6 lb.)	1 teaspoon caraway seeds
	salt

Remove all feathers and hairs, carefully clean and season all over with salt. Sprinkle with caraway seeds and place on a baking tin. Add a few spoons of hot water before putting in the oven so that the skin can steam and give off fat, particularly if the goose is very fat. Roast slowly and when basting prick the surface to let the fat flow out better. First roast with the back upwards and then turn over. When the goose is tender and a good golden colour, remove from the oven, cut into portions and serve with dumplings (see p. 96) and stewed cabbage (see p. 126). A young goose takes about 1 hour to roast, an older, fattened one 2 hours or more.

BREAST OF FATTENED GOOSE WITH GARLIC

1 breast (about 1 lb.)   2 garlic cloves
2 oz. dripping   salt

If the goose is too fat, the fat should be stripped off. A whole layer of fat and skin is thus obtained which can be rendered down. Remove the meat from the breast, rub with crushed garlic and salt, and place in the oven with some dripping. Cook until tender and serve with rice.

GOOSE GIBLETS WITH CAULIFLOWER

giblets from 1 goose   1 cauliflower
3 oz. root vegetables   pinch of mace
   (carrot, celeriac, parsley)   a little soup extract
1 oz. butter   lemon rind
1 oz. plain flour   salt

Clean the giblets and place in boiling water. Add the chopped vegetables and simmer till tender. Make a light roux in a pot, pour over the stock from the giblets, mix well and cook for about 20 minutes. Season with salt, a pinch of mace and lemon rind. Boil the cauliflower separately. Remove the meat from the bones, cut into small pieces and heat together with cauliflower fleurettes in the sauce. Serve with noodles or rice.

ROAST GOOSE LIVER

liver from fattened goose   1 oz. almonds
   (about 1 lb.)   salt
1 gill goose fat

Blanch the almonds and cut them into tiny strips. Poke them into the liver, place it on a baking dish and pour over the fat. Roast it slowly for 30—40 minutes. Cut the hot liver into slices, season with salt and serve with mashed potatoes. An excellent spread is obtained by pouring a spoonful of goose fat over the cooked liver and allowing to cool.

PATE FROM GOOSE LIVER AND GIBLETS

giblets from 1 goose   *Seasoning:* pepper
1 small goose liver   allspice
8 oz. pork   ginger
1 egg   thyme
1 tablespoon breadcrumbs   bay leaf
                                   salt

Clean the giblets and boil till nearly tender. Remove the meat from the bones, mince it together with the liver and pork. Add the egg and seasoning to the mixture and thicken it slightly with breadcrumbs. Pile the mixture into a pudding bowl and steam for about 1 hour.

STUFFED NECK OF GOOSE

1 neck of goose	4 tablespoons milk
½ small goose liver	4 tablespoons breadcrumbs
8 oz. pork	lemon rind
2 tablespoons goose fat	salt

Clean the neck well and singe off the hairs. Mince the pork and liver, add a pinch of grated lemon rind and a few breadcrumbs soaked in milk. The mixture must be thick. Carefully stuff it into the skin of the neck and secure at both ends. Boil in water for about 1 hour, or roast it together with the goose. When cool, cut the neck into slices and serve with bread or hot with potatoes and salad.

GOOSE BLOOD

blood from 1 goose	1 onion
2 tablespoons goose fat	caraway seeds
4 tablespoons milk	salt

Place the blood in a pot, add a little milk and mix well. Fry the finely chopped onion in the fat, add the blood, salt and a few ground caraway seeds, and stir over a moderate flame until cooked. Serve with potatoes and stewed cabbage (see p. 126).

TURKEY WITH CHESTNUT STUFFING

1 turkey	*Stuffing:* 1 lb. bread rolls
4 oz. bacon	4 oz. bacon
4 oz. butter	4 oz. butter
salt	4 eggs
	4 oz. chestnuts
	1 pint milk
	breadcrumbs
	nutmeg
	mace
	parsley

Clean the turkey well and draw strips of bacon through the breast. Fill the breast and inside with stuffing, prepared as follows. Cut the bacon into small pieces and fry slightly. Place the cut up bread rolls in a bowl. Pour over them the eggs beaten with the milk and add the bacon and lukewarm, melted butter, salt, pinch of mace, finely chopped parsley and a pinch of nutmeg. Peel the chestnuts, boil until soft, chop up very finely or mince and add to the rest of the mixture. If the stuffing is too thin, add a few breadcrumbs. Stuff the mixture into the turkey. Place the bird, stuffed side upwards, in a large baking tin with some melted butter and roast slowly for 1—2 hours, basting at intervals with a little water, so that it should not dry out. When carving make sure that each person gets a piece of dark and a piece of light meat and a portion of stuffing.

ROAST PHEASANT

1 pheasant (3—4 lb.)	1 onion
2 oz. bacon	2 juniper berries
2 oz. butter	pepper, allspice
salt	

Clean the pheasant and remove all hairs, wipe, season with salt, thread a few pieces of bacon through the breast and place with slices of onion and the seasoning in a baking tin. During roasting, the top should be well basted to prevent it drying out. Roast for about 1 hour, according to the size and age of the bird. Serve with fried potatoes and stewed cabbage (see p. 126).

PARTRIDGE WITH BACON

2 partridges	1 onion
3 oz. bacon	2 peppercorns or juniper
2 oz. butter	berries
1 teaspoon plain flour	salt

Clean the partridges, wipe well and season with salt. Truss the legs with skewers or wrap each bird in two thick slices of bacon and secure with thread. Melt the butter in a baking tin, add the chopped onion and birds and roast for about 45 minutes until tender. Dredge the juice with plain flour, add a little water and boil. Serve with potatoes and stewed red cabbage (see p. 126).

RABBIT IN RED PEPPER SAUCE

1 back portion of rabbit (about 3 lb.)
5 oz. butter
1 teaspoon flour
1 gill sour cream

1 onion
½ teaspoon sweet red pepper
salt

Clean the rabbit and cut into portions, season with salt and fry quickly in fat with fried onion and red pepper. Add a little water and simmer till tender. Then remove meat, thicken the liquid with flour mixed with the cream and cook well. Return the meat to the strained sauce to heat through. Serve with dumplings or rice.

RABBIT OR HARE WITH ONION

1 back portion of rabbit or hare (about 3 lb.)
2 oz. butter
1 onion

1 tablespoon plain flour
1 bay leaf
a little vinegar
salt

Clean the rabbit or hare and thread strips of bacon through the flesh. Fry the chopped onion in the butter and add the meat, and a bay leaf. Cook in the oven, adding a little water at intervals and basting. Remove the tender meat, dredge the juice with a teaspoon of flour, add a little water and cook for a few minutes. Season with salt and a drop of vinegar.

HARE WITH CREAM SAUCE

1 back portion of hare (about 3 lb.)
2 oz. bacon
3 oz. butter
6 oz. root vegetables (1 carrot,
    piece of celeriac and parsley)
2 tablespoons plain flour
1 pint sour cream

1 onion
6 peppercorns
¼ teaspoon allspice
1 bay leaf
lemon (vinegar)
salt

Wash and skin the back portion of a hare. Draw strips of bacon through flesh and season with salt. Fry the chopped vegetables and onion in the butter, add the seasoning and then the meat. Cook in the oven slowly for about 1 hour, adding a little water and basting at intervals. When the meat is tender, remove it from the baking tin and cut into portions. Mix the cream and flour and add it to the sauce together with the lemon rind and cook well for 20 minutes. The sauce, which should be brownish and thick, should be passed through a sieve together with the vegetables. Season with salt and a little lemon juice to taste. Serve with dumplings and cranberries.

JUGGED HARE

1 front portion of hare (about 2 lb.)	*Seasoning:*	4 peppercorns
3 oz. bacon		pinch allspice
2 oz. butter		½ bay leaf
1 teaspoon sugar		lemon rind
1 onion		
lemon juice	*Roux:*	1 oz. butter
salt		1 tablespoon plain flour

Clean the front portion of a hare, the lungs and heart, and wash well. Cut the flesh into portions. Fry the bacon in a casserole, add the butter and onion and allow it to brown slightly. Add the salted meat, all the seasoning, a little water and cover. Simmer until the meat is tender. Prepare a light brown roux, dilute it with the stock from the hare, add 1 teaspoon burnt sugar and pass the sauce through the sieve. Add more salt and a little lemon juice to taste. Serve with dumplings or potatoes.

RABBIT PASTE

1 skinned rabbit (2—3 lb.)	1 onion
4 oz. calves' liver	a little anchovy paste
3 oz. bacon	*Seasoning:* pepper
3 oz. butter	thyme
3 oz. carrot, celeriac and	bay leaf
parsley root	ginger

Fry the chopped onion and bacon in butter till golden brown. Add the washed, chopped meat and vegetables and simmer till tender. Then remove the meat from the bones, mince finely together with the liver and add salt, seasoning and a little anchovy paste. Steam the mixture in a pudding bowl for about 1 hour.

MINCED HARE

1 front portion of hare	about 2 oz. breadcrumbs
(about 2 lb.)	2 teaspoons plain flour
8 oz. fat pork	1 onion
2 eggs	pepper
3 oz. bacon	salt
2 tablespoons dripping or lard	

Boil the meat from the hare in water, remove from bones and mince finely with the pork. Lightly fry the chopped bacon, add the chopped onion and fry till golden brown. Add to the minced meat and eggs, season with salt and pepper and thicken with a teaspoon of plain flour and a few breadcrumbs. Form the mixture into a long roll, and cook in the oven together with the dripping for about 1 hour. Dredge the juice with 1 teaspoon flour and boil for a few minutes. Serve with boiled potatoes and cranberries. It can also be served cold with bread.

VENISON SCHNITZELS AU NATUREL

4 slices from haunch of venison (1 lb.)
1 tablespoon oil
Worcester sauce
pepper
salt

Piquant butter: 1 tablespoon butter
½ small onion
1 anchovy
piece pickled cucumber
½ teaspoon capers
parsley
small piece lemon rind
small piece garlic (optional)

Finely chop all the ingredients for the piquant butter and beat into the butter. Form the mixture into a long roll and leave in a cold place to harden. Beat the slices of venison with a mallet, wipe them with oil and secure with small skewers to prevent them curling during cooking. Season with salt and a little pepper and fry them quickly in oil on both sides. Place the hot schnitzels on a plate, decorate with a slice of piquant butter and serve very hot garnished with potatoes. The butter melts on the meat and gives it a piquant taste.

ROAST VENISON AU NATUREL

2 lb. haunch of venison
2 oz. bacon
3 oz. butter
1 teaspoon flour

1 onion
2 juniper berries
salt

Wash the meat and thread strips of bacon through the flesh. Fry rapidly in butter then add the chopped onion, salt and juniper berries and cook in the oven, adding a little water at intervals. Remove the meat when tender, dredge the liquid with flour and mix well. Cook for a few minutes. Serve with potatoes, rice or dumplings.

VENISON WITH CREAM SAUCE

2 lb. haunch of venison
3 oz. butter
2 oz. bacon
1 pint sour cream
1 onion
1 tablespoon root vegetables,
    chopped

2 tablespoons flour
½ bay leaf
4 peppercorns,
allspice
pinch sugar
lemon juice or vinegar
salt

Wipe the haunch of venison well, draw strips of bacon
through the flesh and season with salt. Melt the butter,
slightly fry the onion and root vegetables, then add the
seasoning and meat and fry quickly till the meat changes
colour. Add a little water and cook in the oven till tender.
Remove the meat and cut into portions. Thicken the sauce
with flour mixed in the sour cream and cook for a few minutes.
Then pass it through a sieve and add a little vinegar or lemon
juice. Serve with dumplings.

VENISON HASH

1½ lb. shoulder of venison
2 oz. bacon
2 oz. butter
1 teaspoon plain flour
3 oz. mushrooms
piece of celeriac

1 onion
pinch ginger
salt
a few drops of Worcester sauce
lemon juice

Cut the meat into pieces and fry with the bacon and chopped
celeriac and mushrooms. Add a little water and the seasoning
and simmer till tender. Remove the meat and pass through
a mincer. Make a light roux from the butter and flour, add
the liquid from the meat and cook for a few minutes. Add the
minced meat and season with salt, Worcester sauce and
a little lemon juice (optional). Serve the hash with potatoes
and a green salad.

STUFFED SNAILS

16 snails
2 eggs
4 oz. butter
2 tablespoons milk
about 3 tablespoons bread-
    crumbs

3 anchovies
onion
parsley
salt and pepper
a piece of carrot, celeriac
    and parsley root

Scrub the snails and wash well. Throw them into boiling
water and cook for about 10 minutes. Take out of the water
and remove the shells, cut off the soft end and pull out
entrails. Rub the flesh with salt and then wash well in several
lots of water. Place in a pot together with the root vegetables
and onion and cook for about 3 hours. When tender cut the
flesh into tiny pieces and add to the stuffing, which should
be made as follows. Beat the butter and anchovies, add the
eggs, breadcrumbs and finely chopped parsley. Boil the shells
and wash well. Form the stuffing into small rolls and push
into the shells leaving a little hanging out. Arrange them on
a fireproof dish and bake for about 15 minutes. The shells
can also be filled with a stuffing prepared from pieces of
cooked goose liver.

CARP IN BUTTER

4 portions carp (about 2 lb.)
4 oz. butter
lemon slices

parsley
salt

Clean the carp, season with salt, dredge with flour and fry
quickly in butter. Place on a plate, pour over the butter from
the frying pan, decorate with finely chopped parsley and
some slices of lemon. Serve with potatoes.

CARP WITH ANCHOVIES

4 portions carp (about 2 lb.)   1 wineglass white wine
3 oz. butter   lemon
2 anchovies   pepper
1 teaspoon plain flour   salt

Fry the fish in part of the butter. Beat the rest of the butter
with the finely chopped anchovies. Remove the fish from the
pan, add the flour, anchovy butter, seasoning, a few drops of
lemon juice and wine and cook for a few minutes. Return the
fish to the piquant sauce and serve with potatoes.

DEVILLED CARP (CHRISTMAS DISH)

3 lb. carp   1 tablespoon chopped almonds
2 oz. butter   1 tablespoon sultanas
1 carrot   1 tablespoon sugar
piece of celeriac   2 tablespoons vinegar
½ small parsley root   1 bay leaf
½ onion   5 peppercorns
1 pint brown ale   pinch allspice
1 cup grated gingerbread   pinch thyme
1 tablespoon redcurrant jelly   lemon rind
   or handful of prunes   salt

Keep the blood from a freshly caught carp and dilute with
the vinegar. Clean the fish, cut into portions and fry in the
butter. Remove the fish and prepare the sauce. Fry the vegetables and onion in the butter, add the seasoning, grated
gingerbread, blood and vinegar, beer and lemon rind and
cook all together till the sauce thickens. Pass it through
a sieve, add the redcurrant jelly, sultanas and peeled and
chopped almonds, and a little sugar, vinegar and salt to taste.
Return the fish to this sweet-sour sauce to heat through.
The best results are obtained if the fish and sauce are prepared
the day before and then only heated up.

PIKE WITH PIQUANT SAUCE

1 small pike (2 lb.)	1 teaspoon grated horseradish
4 oz. butter	pinch red pepper
1 tablespoon plain flour	1 teaspoon French mustard
small piece onion	salt and pepper

Season pieces of fish with salt, pepper and red pepper, dredge with flour and fry in the butter. Add teaspoon of mustard and grated horseradish to the juice, sprinkle with flour, add a little water and cook for a few minutes. Serve with potatoes.

BOILED TROUT

1½ lb. trout	1 lemon
4 oz. butter	salt

Clean the fish and simmer in salted water. Carefully remove it, pour over the hot melted butter and serve with slices of lemon.

FISH IN ASPIC

2 lb. fish (carp, pike etc.)	5 peppercorns
2 egg whites	pinch allspice
2 oz. gelatine	½ bay leaf
1 gill vinegar	salt
3 oz. root vegetables	1 onion

Boil the cleaned and chopped vegetables, salt and seasoning. Cut the fish into portions, place in a pot skin upwards and pour over boiling vinegar to make the skin blue. Then carefully add the fish and vinegar to the boiling vegetables and cook for about 10 minutes. Carefully remove the fish. Sieve about 1¾ pints of the fish stock into a pot, add the gelatine which has been dissolved in a little cold water and gently heat, mixing all the time, but do not boil. Add the beaten egg whites and whisk until they congeal. Strain through a jelly bag, pour the clear liquid over the fish and allow to set. The fish can be arranged in a bowl with slices of egg, carrot, paprika etc. and the jelly spooned onto it and then allowed to set.

MARINADED EEL

1 eel (about 2 lb.)	2 tablespoons flour
¼ pint mayonnaise	lemon
3 tablespoons oil	pepper and salt

Skin the eel, season with salt and pepper, dredge with flour and fry quickly in the oil till golden brown. Then cut it into small portions and pour over the marinade made from the mayonnaise, the remains of the oil in which it has been fried and a little water. Add a little lemon juice and more salt if necessary. Leave the eel in the marinade in a cool place till the next day.

Many and varied are the sauces in Czech cooking. Hot sauces are served particularly with boiled beef but also with boiled pork (pig's head, smoked meat), fish and vegetables.

Vegetables such as onion, dill, chives, horse-radish, tomatoes and cucumbers form the basis for most of the hot sauces. They are thickened with a light or a dark roux and diluted with meat or vegetable stock, milk or cream.

Cream sauces are a special favourite and are served with bread dumplings. Vegetable sauces are served with potatoes, rice or pasta.

Apart from cream, egg yolks and fresh butter are sometimes used to improve sauces.

The basis for cold sauces is mayonnaise, prepared from fresh yolks and oil. By adding different flavourings and coloured ingredients to enhance the appearance and taste we obtain a number of different cold sauces.

Otherwise cold sauces are only made as marinades—an example is the typical horse-radish sauce, made with grated apple or carrot, which is served with boiled ribs of beef or boiled pig's head. Cold sauces are served both with cold boiled meats or fried dishes (fried vegetables, cheese, meat, poultry, fish) or with boiled vegetables, poultry and fish.

TOMATO SAUCE

1 oz. butter	small piece bay leaf
1 oz. flour	salt
1 oz. onion	1 teaspoon sugar
8 oz. tomatoes or 2 tablespoons	vinegar
tomato purée	pinch allspice
pinch thyme	½ pint stock

Fry the chopped onion lightly in butter. Add the flour and make a light roux. Dilute with water or meat stock, bring to the boil stirring well. Add the washed, sliced tomatoes and seasoning and cook for about 10 minutes. Pass through a sieve and season with salt, sugar and vinegar to taste. If tomato purée is used, first make a light roux, add the liquid to make a thick sauce and only add the purée at the end.

MUSHROOM SAUCE

8 oz. fresh mushrooms or	1 oz. flour
½ oz. dried mushrooms	caraway seeds
1 oz. onion	parsley
1 oz. butter	½ pint stock

Peel and wash the mushrooms and cut into slices. Fry the chopped onion in butter, add the flour and liquid and bring to the boil stirring well. Add the mushrooms, a few caraway seeds and salt and simmer till soft. Before serving add the finely chopped parsley. If dried mushrooms are used, first wash them and then soak them for 30 minutes in cold water. Then chop them, simmer with the caraway seeds and finally add to the sauce.

CREAMY MUSHROOM SAUCE

½ pint stock
8 oz. fresh mushrooms
1½ oz. butter
1 onion

1 oz. flour
salt and pepper
1 gill cream
lemon juice
1 egg yolk (optional)

Cut the cleaned mushrooms into slices and simmer in a little fat until soft. Boil the chopped onion, seasoning with salt and pepper. Make a light roux from the butter and flour, dilute with stock from the onion and simmer for a few minutes. Add the cooked mushrooms and cream and a few drops of lemon juice. An egg yolk may be added, in which case the sauce should only be slightly reheated but not allowed to boil.

MUSHROOM SAUCE WITH WINE

½ pint stock
1 gill white wine
8 oz. field mushrooms

lemon juice
1 oz. fat
1 oz. flour

Clean and slice the mushrooms and simmer in the fat. When all the juice has evaporated, dredge with flour, allow to brown slightly and add the stock. Stir well and add the wine. Boil for a few minutes and then add a few drops of lemon juice.

DILL SAUCE

2 egg yolks	1 tablespoon chopped dill
1 pint cream or milk	salt
1 oz. flour	$\frac{1}{8}$ oz. butter
1 oz. sugar	1 dessertspoon vinegar

Whisk together the cream, flour, salt and sugar and bring to the boil. Simmer for about 15 minutes. Add the yolks, whisked separately in a little cold sauce, and the chopped dill, boiled with vinegar. Before serving add the melted butter to the sauce.

COLD CHIVE SAUCE

2 eggs	3 tablespoons oil
2 oz. breadcrumbs	1 tablespoon chopped parsley
4 tablespoons milk	vinegar
	salt

Hard-boil the eggs and take out the yolks. Pass through a sieve together with the breadcrumbs which have been soaked in a little milk. Add the oil, a few drops at a time, season with salt and a few drops of vinegar and finally add the chopped parsley.

COOKED MAYONNAISE

4 egg yolks	2 oz. butter
½ pint beef soup	pinch sugar
1 teaspoon flour	salt and pepper
½ teaspoon French mustard	vinegar or lemon juice

Season the soup with salt and add the egg yolks, flour, a few drops of vinegar, pepper, sugar, chopped butter and mustard. Whisk well. Heat slowly, stirring all the time until the mixture begins to thicken. Remove from stove and stir until quite cold. This mayonnaise is used for making potato and vegetable salads, with boiled fish, meat or vegetables.

TARTARE SAUCE

2 egg yolks	rind of ½ lemon
½ pint oil	½ oz. onion
salt	½ teaspoon capers
1 tablespoon lemon juice	1 anchovy
	1 pickled cucumber

Separate the egg yolks from the whites and place in a china bowl. Add a pinch of salt and whisk well. Add the oil, a few drops at a time, stirring continually. When the mayonnaise begins to thicken the oil may be added in a thin stream. When the mixture has thickened add a few drops of lemon juice or vinegar and the rest of the ingredients: finely chopped onion, finely grated lemon rind, capers, anchovy from which the bones have been removed and chopped cucumber. Leave for a few hours to allow the different ingredients to permeate the sauce. Tartare sauce is served with boiled and roast meat, fish and fried dishes.

COTTAGE CHEESE MAYONNAISE

4 oz. cottage cheese
2 egg yolks
3—4 tablespoons oil
1 teaspoon vinegar

pinch sugar
½ teaspoon French mustard
salt and pepper
pinch caraway seeds

Pass the cottage cheese through a fine sieve and mix with the yolks. Alternately add milk and a few drops of oil, thus making a thick sauce similar to mayonnaise. Season with salt and pepper, a little ground caraway seed, French mustard, sugar, vinegar or a little lemon juice. Serve with boiled meat or fish. It can also be used in vegetable salads.

PLUM 'KLEVERA'

6 lb. plums
1 lb. sugar

1 gill rum
pinch benzoic acid

Wash the plums and pass them through a meat mincer. Cook rapidly for about 30 minutes. Then add the sugar and boil again for about 15 minutes. Remove from stove, add some good rum in which a pinch of benzoic acid has been dissolved. Pour into pots and cover. Klevera is poured over fruit dumplings, spread on yeast pancakes and 'vdolky' doughnuts and served as a sauce with puddings.

BILBERRY SAUCE

1 lb. bilberries	1 teaspoon potato flour
2 oz. sugar	½ pint milk
1 oz. butter	

Wash and pick over the bilberries. Place in a pot together
with half the milk and the butter and sugar and boil till soft.
Mix the potato flour with the rest of the milk and add to the
bilberries. Simmer for a few minutes, stirring all the time.
This sauce is used on yeast pancakes, yeast dumplings, and
'vdolky' doughnuts or for pouring over puddings and
soufflés.

HORSE-RADISH AND APPLE

1 oz. horse-radish	salt
3 tablespoons cold beef stock (or water)	vinegar to taste
2 apples	pinch sugar

Wash the horse-radish, scrape and grate finely. Add the
peeled and grated apples, a pinch of salt, the stock and a few
drops of vinegar or lemon juice. The vinegar or lemon juice
must be added as soon as the horse-radish and apple have
been grated or they will turn brown.

Grated carrot may be added instead of apple, in which case
the sauce should be made with lemon juice.

This condiment is served with boiled meat, particularly ribs
of beef, boiled pig's head or boiled smoked meat.

If it is served with boiled fish or game 2 tablespoons thickly
whipped cream may be added instead of part of the stock.

POTATOES, DUMPLINGS, PASTA, RICE, LENTILS

Filling dishes, such as dumplings, are a great favourite with the Czechs. There are a number of different types of dumplings ranging from the ordinary bread and potato dumplings to those made with eggs and flour, which are more like soufflés. The shapes, too, differ from type to type. Some are made into long rolls, which are then cut across in slices. Others are boiled in the form of small balls. They are cooked either in water or steamed, rolled up in a napkin. Yeast, baking powder or whisked white of egg is used to make them light. They are mixed with a little water, milk or soda water.

Other favourite dishes are rice and groats. Vegetable dishes, which are less filling, are served with fried potatoes, noodle cakes, etc.

The favourite accompaniment to smoked meat and cheese is dark rye bread or a crisp roll. The bakeries produce a large assortment of bread and rolls which used to be baked at home. Even now, if a housewife wishes to serve guests with particularly small tasty rolls, filled or with a spread, she makes them at home.

With a good recipe the preparation of dumplings is not difficult. They must, however, be light and well salted. We hope you will enjoy them.

POTATO CRISPS

2 lb. potatoes   5 garlic cloves
3 oz. dripping or butter   salt

Scrub the potatoes and cut them into thin slices. Arrange on a baking tin and bake in a moderate oven. When they are slightly browned on one side carefully turn them over and brown on the other side. Crush the garlic in a bowl together with some salt and dripping or butter. Add the potatoes and shake well. Serve hot with tea or as an accompaniment to vegetables.

FINE MASHED POTATOES

2 lb. potatoes   1 egg yolk
½ pint milk   ½ onion
3 oz. butter   salt

Pour boiling salted water over peeled and halved potatoes and cook till soft. Mash well or pass through a sieve. Add the milk and egg yolk, a knob of fresh butter and mix well. Sprinkle finely chopped and fried onion and a little melted butter over the mash. Serve with fried meat or frankfurters.

POTATO AND GROAT MASH

2 lb. potatoes	2 oz. butter
4 oz. groats	1 onion
1 gill milk	salt

Pour boiling water over the groats, add a small knob of fat and boil till soft. Cook the peeled potatoes in salted water till soft, drain and mash with a little milk. Add the groats. Sprinkle the mash with fried onion and melted butter. Serve with salad or as an accompaniment to smoked meat or frankfurters.

SHKUBANKY (POTATO CAKES AND POPPY-SEED)

2 lb. potatoes	2 oz. poppy-seed
5 oz. plain flour	2 oz. sugar
3 oz. lard	salt

Peel and quarter the potatoes, cover with boiling salted water and cook till nearly soft. Then drain off the water into a bowl. Mash the potatoes, and make several holes in the mash with the end of a wooden spoon. The holes should reach right to the bottom of the pot. Fill them with the flour and pour on about half of the water, which should be boiling. Leave covered on the edge of the stove for about 30 minutes. Then pour off the excess water and beat the mixture with a wooden spoon till smooth. The mixture should be very stiff. Using a spoon dipped in hot lard place spoonfuls of the mixture on a plate. Sprinkle with ground poppy-seeds or grated gingerbread, sugar and lard. An alternative is to sprinkle the shkubanky with grated cottage cheese and melted butter. Shkubanky are also excellent fried (see p. 91).

SHKUBANKY FRY

shkubanky dough from 2 lb.   breadcrumbs
   potatoes (see p. 90)   flour
1 egg   5 oz. fat for frying

Form small cakes from the shkubanky dough, dip in flour, egg and breadcrumbs and fry till golden brown. These are a filling accompaniment to spinach or peas.

POTATO DUMPLINGS FROM COOKED POTATOES

1½ lb. potatoes   2 tablespoons semolina
2 eggs   8 oz. coarse flour or 4 oz. plain
2 tablespoons vinegar   flour and 4 oz. fine semolina
salt

Use potatoes which have been boiled and peeled the day before. Grate them and add a little salt, the eggs and vinegar, semolina and flour. Knead the dough till it is firm. Do not leave it to stand or it will get too soft. Form the dough into four rolls and throw into boiling salted water. After a few minutes they should rise to the surface. Cook them for about 20 minutes, then carefully take them out of the water and cut into slices with a sharp knife. Serve with roast meat.

SHAGGY DUMPLINGS FROM RAW POTATOES

1½ lb. potatoes	2 oz. lard or dripping
1 egg	salt
8 oz. fine semolina	

Peel the potatoes and grate them finely or pulp them in an emulsifier. Drain off part of the water. Mix the pulp with salt, beaten egg and the fine semolina to a soft dough. Using a spoon dipped in hot water cut out knobs of dough and throw them into boiling water, taking care that they do not stick to the bottom of the pot. Boil for about 8 minutes, remove from the water and place in a pot with the melted lard or dripping. Shaggy dumplings are served with pork or bacon and hot sauerkraut or with roast pork.

POTATO CONES WITH FRIED BREADCRUMBS

1½ lb. potatoes	3 oz. lard or dripping
12 oz. fine semolina	3 tablespoons breadcrumbs
1 egg	salt

Use potatoes which have been boiled and peeled the day before. Grate them onto a board, add the flour, salt, egg and knead into a stiff dough. Form the dough into a long roll and then cut into small pieces, shaped like small cones. Boil in salt water for about 4 minutes. Remove from the water, drain well and place in a baking dish together with the fried breadcrumbs. Shake well so that the cones are covered all over with the breadcrumbs. Serve with lettuce or as an accompaniment to roast meat, vegetables etc. The boiled cones may also be served without the breadcrumbs but sprinkled with ground poppyseeds or grated gingerbread and sugar.

POTATO DUMPLINGS WITH SMOKED MEAT

1½ lb. potatoes　　1 egg
8 oz. smoked meat　3 oz. butter or dripping
8 oz. fine semolina　salt

Boil the potatoes, then peel them and mash them on a board.
Add the egg, salt and semolina and knead into a stiff, elastic
dough. Flour the board, roll out the dough and cut into small
squares. Finely chop the cooked smoked meat and place a
little on each piece of dough. Join up the corners of each
square and form into a small dumpling. Cook in boiling
water for about 10 minutes. Drain off the water, prick with
a fork, place on a plate and pour over the melted butter or
dripping. Serve with hot cabbage or a vegetable salad.

POTATO PANCAKES

2 lb. potatoes	a few spoonfuls milk
1 egg	1 garlic clove
4 oz. plain flour	salt
5 oz. lard for frying	

Peel the potatoes and grate them finely. Then season with salt, sprinkle on a little milk and add the egg and enough flour to make a thick batter. Ladle small amounts into hot lard, pat out into pancakes with a knife, and fry quickly on both sides till golden. Remove from pan and smear thinly with crushed garlic. Chopped chives or a pinch of marjoram are sometimes added to the batter.

SIMPLE POTATO SALAD

2 lb. potatoes	*Marinade:*	4 tablespoons oil
2 eggs		1 tablespoon French mustard
2 pickled gherkins		tard
1 large onion		a little vinegar
1 paprika		pinch salt and sugar

Cook the potatoes, then peel off the skin and allow to cool. Cut into slices, mix with the chopped onion, gherkins, paprika and sweet-sour marinade. Arrange slices of hard-boiled eggs on the top of the salad.

SPECIAL POTATO SALAD

2 lb. potatoes	1 tablespoon chopped carrot
4 oz. ham or salami	1 tablespoon chopped pars-
2 eggs	ley root
3 pickled gherkins	1 large onion
1 gill green peas	¼ pint mayonnaise
2 tablespoons chopped cele-	lemon juice or vinegar
riac	

Cook the potatoes until they are just soft but not mushy. Then peel them and cut into small cubes. Boil the vegetables. Chop the onion, gherkins, ham and hard-boiled eggs. Put all the ingredients into a large bowl and bind with mayonnaise to which a little lemon juice or vinegar has been added.

POTATO SALAD WITH SAUERKRAUT

2 lb. potatoes	*Marinade:*	3 tablespoons oil
5 oz. sauerkraut		½ teaspoon caraway seeds
1 onion		a little vinegar
		sugar and salt to season

Slice the peeled and cooked potatoes while still hot and mix with finely chopped sauerkraut. Add the marinade and finely chopped onion. Mix all together carefully so that the slices of potatoes remain whole. Serve warm with smoked meat.

CZECH BREAD DUMPLINGS

1 lb. coarse flour *or* 8 oz. plain
    flour and 8 oz. fine semolina
about 1 pint milk
4 bread rolls (about 7 oz.)

2 egg yolks
½ teaspoon salt
1 teaspoon fat

Weigh the flour into a deep mixing bowl, add the salt and milk mixed with the yolks. Beat the dough with a wooden spoon until it is soft and bubbly. Cut the rolls into cubes (rolls a day old are best), lightly fry them in a small piece of butter and add them to the dough. Flour a board, turn part of the dough onto it and form it into a roll. Throw the roll into boiling water in a large pot so that it has enough room to float. When the water again comes to the boil, add another roll. The dumplings should boil for about 30 minutes. Remove from the water and cut into slices. These bread dumplings are served, for example, with roast pork, goose, duck, chicken in paprika sauce and with all meat dishes having thick sauces, especially creamy sauces.

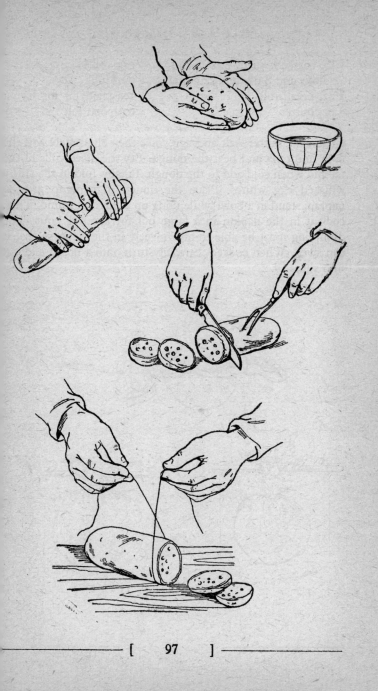

RICH DUMPLINGS

1 lb. coarse flour or 8 oz. plain
   flour and 8 oz. fine semolina
7 oz. bread rolls
4 oz. butter

4 egg yolks
½ pint milk
1 teaspoon fat for frying
½ teaspoon salt

Cream the butter, salt and egg yolks then alternately add the flour and milk and beat the dough. Fry the diced rolls in the fat and when cold add to the dough. Finally fold in the stiffly whisked egg whites. Place the dough in a damp greased napkin, stand in a bowl while tying up to make it round. Then cook it in the napkin in a large pot for about 1 hour. The dumpling must be able to move freely in the water so that it can swell. When cooked, carefully turn onto a board and cut into slices.

RICH DUMPLINGS (ANOTHER VERSION)

10 bread rolls (about 1 lb.)	1 pint milk
3 tablespoons fine semolina	3 tablespoons butter
3 egg yolks	salt

Use rolls which are a day old, cut them into cubes and sprinkle with milk in which the melted butter and eggs have been whisked. Add the flour and turn onto a floured board. Form into small round dumplings by firmly pressing between the palms of the hand. Then throw them into boiling salted water and cook for about 20 minutes. Remove from water and slightly tear apart with a fork to allow the steam to escape. Pour over a little butter or dripping and serve with roast or braised meat.

SEMOLINA DUMPLINGS

8 oz. semolina	3 oz. bread rolls
2 eggs	salt
½ pint milk	

Boil the semolina in milk seasoned with salt, stirring well. When the mixture thickens remove from stove and allow to cool. Add the eggs and diced rolls. Turn the dough into a damp napkin and tie just above the dough. Cook in boiling water for about 45 minutes. Then carefully turn onto a board and cut into slices.

SAVOURY SEMOLINA PUDDING

2 oz. semolina
1 pint milk
1 tablespoon butter

1 onion
pinch salt

Lightly fry the semolina in part of the butter till golden. Then pour on the milk, add the salt and cook for 10 minutes stirring all the time. Serve sprinkled with fried onion and melted butter. This dish is eaten with vegetables or salad.

BOILED RICE

8 oz. rice
1 oz. lard or dripping

1 onion
1 clove

Pick over the rice and wash in cold water. Fry in the fat together with a little salt. Add the onion into which the clove has been stuck and pour on water until the rice is covered with a layer of liquid 1—2 inches thick.

Another method of boiling rice is as follows. Boil the rice in salt water for about 3 minutes. Then drain it and add to fried onion. After a few minutes add boiling water until the rice is covered with a layer of liquid 1—2 inches thick. Cover the pot and stew for about 20 minutes. Do not stir the rice during cooking; merely shake it lightly. If water has to be added it must be boiling. If the rice is served as an accompaniment place it on the plates with a ladle so that it forms a small mound. Boiled rice may also be eaten as a dish on its own, in which case either 4 oz. chopped smoked meat or 2 oz. grated cheese is added.

PEA PUREE

12 oz. dried peas	*Roux:* 1 oz. dripping
1 gill milk	1 tablespoon flour
salt	*Garnish:* 2 oz. bacon fat
	1 onion

Pick over the peas, wash them and leave to soak overnight in cold water. Cook in the same water until soft. Then pass through a hair sieve or meat mincer. From the dripping and flour prepare a light roux, dilute with milk and mix into the pea purée. Simmer for about 10 minutes. Finally season with salt and sprinkle with fried onion and bacon fat. It may also be garnished with the jelly from pork or goose fat. Serve with sauerkraut salad or pickled cucumbers, or as an accompaniment to smoked meat, ham or sausage.

LENTILS

12 oz. lentils	1 onion
3 oz. lard or dripping	a little vinegar
1 oz. flour	salt

Soak the lentils in water for 24 hours. Then simmer them in the same water till tender. Fry the chopped onion in the lard, add the flour and dilute with a cup of the water in which the lentils have been boiled. Stir well and cook for about 10 minutes. Season with salt, a little vinegar and mix with the lentils. Serve with hard-boiled or fried eggs, or frankfurters.

BEAN SALAD

12 oz. haricot beans	parsley
2 tablespoons oil	pinch sugar
1 onion	salt
vinegar	

Wash the beans and soak them overnight in cold water. Then simmer them in the same water till tender. Drain, place in bowl and pour over marinade made from oil, water, a little vinegar and a pinch of sugar and salt. Sprinkle the top with chopped onion. Serve with cold roast meat.

COTTAGE CHEESE GNOCCHI

1 lb. cottage cheese	2 oz. butter
8 oz. fine semolina	a few breadcrumbs
3—4 eggs	salt

Cream the butter with the yolks and salt. Add the soft cottage cheese, semolina and finally the stiffly whisked whites. Tie up in a damp cloth and steam over a large pot of boiling water, tying the cloth to a wooden spoon placed across the pot. Cook for 45 minutes to 1 hour. Carefully remove from the cloth, allow to solidify and then cut into slices. Sprinkle the slices with fried breadcrumbs and serve with melted butter. They can also be served with melted damson cheese and butter.

PASTA WITH SMOKED MEAT

8 oz. pasta (square noodles)　　1 gill milk
4 oz. smoked meat　　　　　　　1 tablespoon breadcrumbs
2 eggs　　　　　　　　　　　　　salt
2 tablespoons lard or dripping

Boil the pasta in salt water till nearly soft. Drain and add a little fat then allow to cool. Grease a baking tin or fireproof dish with dripping and sprinkle with breadcrumbs. Mix the pasta with chopped smoked meat, place in the baking tin, sprinkle with melted fat and bake in a moderate oven. After about 15 minutes pour over the beaten eggs and milk and bake until a crisp crust is formed. Serve with lettuce or some other salad.

HOME-MADE NOODLES

8 oz. plain flour　　　ground poppy-seed and sugar
2 eggs　　　　　　　　1 cup water
3 oz. butter　　　　　salt

Sieve the flour onto a board, make a small well in the centre and pour in the eggs beaten in a little water. Work the liquid carefully into the flour and knead into an elastic dough until it no longer sticks to the board. Roll out into two very thin pieces. Allow to dry, turning over after a time to dry them evenly. Then cut the dough into strips, place these on top of each other and cut across into noodles. Cook the noodles in a sufficient amount of boiling salt water for about 10—15 minutes. Serve with stewed chicken, veal in paprika sauce or as a dish on its own, sprinkled with grated cottage cheese or grated hard cheese and salt. It can also be served sweet, garnished with ground poppy-seed and sugar. Home-made noodles can be baked with meat or served sweet with cottage cheese or fruit.

PANCAKES

7 oz. plain flour	about 2 oz. fat for frying
1 pint milk	salt
2 eggs	

Sieve the flour into a bowl, add the milk and egg yolks, season with salt and whisk well. Finally fold in the stiffly whisked egg whites. Fry thin pancakes in a greased frying-pan, roll up and serve with vegetables or salad.

ECONOMICAL BREAD ROLLS

1 lb. plain flour	1 oz. baker's yeast
2 potatoes	1 teaspoon fat
1 egg	thickening made from ½ pint water and
3 tablespoons milk	2 oz. plain flour
salt	

Gently cook the mixed 2 oz. flour and water for the thickening and allow to cool. Sieve 1 lb. plain flour into a bowl, add the cold, boiled and grated potatoes, the yeast which has been left for a time in a little warm milk, and the thickening. Mix into a very stiff dough. Form into small round rolls, place on a greased baking tin and leave to prove for 30 minutes. Brush with beaten egg and sprinkle with salt. Bake in a hot oven till golden. These little rolls can be filled with various spreads.

ROZPEKY (BAKED BALLS)

2 lb. plain flour   1 teaspoon baker's yeast
1 egg yolk   a little milk
3 oz. fat   pinch sugar
    salt

Put the yeast to sponge with a little milk, sugar and flour. Add to the 2 lb. plain flour, together with a pinch of salt, an egg yolk and the melted fat and mix to a soft smooth dough. Leave to rise in a warm place. Then form into small doughnuts, place on a greased tin and again leave to rise for about 15 minutes. Bake in a hot oven. These rozpeky are sometimes served for tea but more frequently as an accompaniment to meat with a sauce, instead of dumplings (e.g. with tomato sauce).

PAVEZKY (FRIED BREAD)

7 oz. bread or rolls   3 oz. fat for frying
1 egg   1 cup milk
breadcrumbs   salt

Cut the bread or rolls into thin slices, moisten each with a little milk, dip in beaten egg and breadcrumbs and fry in fat till golden. Pavezky form a tasty accompaniment to vegetables.

SALT STICKS

1 lb. flour and fine semolina mixed
1 egg
1 gill milk
2 oz. fat

1 oz. baker's yeast
1 lump sugar
caraway seeds
salt

Sieve the flour and semolina into a bowl, add the yeast which has been put to sponge with a little milk and sugar, the egg and melted fat. Mix into a stiff dough and leave for about 1 hour to rise. Roll out long thin sticks from the dough, brush with milk or egg and sprinkle with coarse salt and caraway seeds. Bake in a moderate oven till golden brown. This dough may also be used to make small plaited rolls, caraway trefoil rolls etc.

EGG DISHES

In Czechoslovakia eggs are a favourite dish for breakfast and snacks and often as a main dish for lunch or supper. As an entrée they are most often served with some kind of potato salad or are filled with a piquant mixture. As a main dish eggs are boiled and served with a sauce (dill, chive, mushroom, tomato) or fried and served with vegetables, mashed potato or pulse purées. A quick and tasty supper are scrambled eggs, which in summer time may be made to go further with mushrooms or vegetables (cooked cauliflower, fried paprika and tomato), or eggs with ham or smoked meat.

Eggs form the basis for many other dishes. They are served in the form of savoury or sweet omelettes, pancakes, soufflés, sandwich spreads and puddings. In Czech cooking, eggs also form the main ingredient in many favourite cakes (sponges, choux pastry, etc.) where the stiffly whisked whites are the principal raising agent.

PIQUANT EGGS

8 eggs (2 per person)   2 oz. butter
                          2 oz. grated horse-radish

Place the eggs in boiling water and cook for 4—5 minutes.
Then remove them and submerge for a moment in cold water
so that they are easily peeled, but do not let them cool. Serve
with melted butter and sprinkled with grated horse-radish
or with fried onion. They are also excellent with tartare sauce,
continental mustard or ketchup. Serve with black bread and
butter.

SCRAMBLED EGGS WITH SEMOLINA

2—5 eggs   ½ pint milk
1½ oz. butter   2 tablespoons semolina

Melt the butter in a pan, add the milk in which the semolina has been soaked for about 10 minutes. Stir until the mixture thickens, then add the eggs and continue stirring until the eggs have scrambled. Serve with black bread.

LOST EGGS

4 eggs	½ oz. flour
1 onion	½ pint beef stock
salt	1 cup Madeira
3 oz. mushrooms	nutmeg
2 oz. butter	parsley
1 oz. truffles	4 tablespoons vinegar

Bring 1½ pints water with the vinegar to the boil. Then break one egg after another into a ladle and carefully add to the water which has been removed from the stove for a few minutes. Using a fork scoop the white close up to the yolk and again place on the stove. The eggs are cooked in about 3 minutes. Chop the onion and truffles into small pieces and stew in the butter. When the onion begins to brown add the flour and then dilute with the stock. Whisk the sauce well and cook for a few minutes. Add the seasoning, Madeira, sliced fresh mushrooms and chopped parsley. Pour this sauce over the eggs and serve with potatoes, rice or pasta.

SCRAMBLED EGGS WITH MUSHROOMS

4—6 eggs
1 lb. fresh mushrooms
2 oz. butter

salt
caraway seeds
lemon juice

Clean the mushrooms, cut into slices and stew in about half the fat. Season with salt, a few caraway seeds and a few drops of lemon juice. Beat the eggs with the salt and add to the stewed mushrooms. Mix well until the eggs curdle and before serving add a knob of fresh butter. Serve with bread or potatoes.

SCRAMBLED EGGS WITH VEGETABLES AND CHEESE

6 eggs
2 tablespoons cream
2 oz. butter
4 oz. vegetables (peas, cauliflower,
    beans, asparagus)

2 oz. cheese
French mustard
salt

Melt about half the butter. Whisk the cream and eggs and pour onto the butter. Before the eggs scramble add the cooked, finely chopped vegetables. Mix well together and when the eggs thicken add the rest of the butter, a little French mustard, salt and grated cheese. Serve with bread or potatoes.

SCRAMBLED EGGS AND HAM

6 eggs	parsley or chives
1½ oz. butter	salt
4 oz. ham	6 tablespoons water

Cut the ham finely and fry in the butter. Whisk the eggs in the water, season with salt and add to the ham. Stir until it thickens. Garnish with chopped parsley or chives. Serve with bread or rolls.

EGGS STUFFED WITH ANCHOVIES

6 eggs	2 tablespoons mayonnaise
2 oz. butter	mustard, salt
2 anchovies	parsley

Hard-boil the eggs, cut lengthwise, remove the yolks and beat with the butter and chopped anchovies. After beating for a few minutes add a little French mustard, salt and the mayonnaise. Pile the mixture into a piping bag with a large nozzle and pipe into the halves of the whites. Decorate the top with chopped parsley or capers. Serve with bread or rolls.

EGGS STUFFED WITH HAM

6 eggs   1 anchovy
5 oz. ham   parsley
2 oz. butter   salt and pepper

Hard-boil the eggs and cut lengthwise. Remove the yolks and beat with half the butter. Fry the finely chopped ham in the rest of the butter. Allow to cool and add chopped parsley. Mix the yolks with the chopped anchovy, seasoning and ham. Using wet hands, form the mixture into little balls and place them on the halves of whites. Serve with bread or rolls.

EGGS WITH CHEESE STUFFING

6 eggs   1 oz. butter
3 tablespoons sour cream   chives
2 oz. cheese

Hard-boil the eggs and when cool cut lengthwise. Beat the yolks with the butter, add the grated cheese and thick cream and beat well together. Finally add the finely chopped chives. Pile the mixture into the halves of the whites. Serve garnished with lettuce.

EGGS WITH VEGETABLE STUFFING

6 eggs	green paprika
2 teaspoons mayonnaise	parsley
pickled gherkin	

Hard-boil the eggs and when cool cut lengthwise. Remove the yolks and beat with the mayonnaise and finely chopped vegetables. Pile the mixture into the halves of the whites and serve on a bed of lettuce, with bread or rolls.

FRIED SOFT-BOILED EGGS

4 eggs	1 egg and 3 oz. breadcrumbs for coating
4 oz. fat	salt
1 oz. flour	

Soft-boil the four eggs until the white is firm and then remove the shell. Allow to cool, then dip in seasoned flour, egg and breadcrumbs and fry till golden in hot fat. Serve with raw or cooked vegetable salad. The eggs may also be wrapped in slices of ham, salami or very thin fillets of meat and then dipped in flour, egg and breadcrumbs and fried.

EGGS WITH LENTILS

10 oz. lentils	4—6 eggs
2 oz. lard or dripping	1 oz. butter
1 oz. flour	salt
½ onion	vinegar

Place small knobs of butter in the pans of an egg-poacher and when it melts break an egg into each pan. Cook slowly. When the white sets, carefully remove. Serve with lentils. To cook the lentils, soak in water for 3 to 4 hours then cook in the same water till soft. Fry the finely chopped onion in the lard or dripping, dredge with flour and dilute with the water from the lentils. Stir well and add to the lentils. Add a few drops of vinegar to taste, and serve garnished with melted fat and the eggs.

ANCHOVY EGGS (HOT)

6 eggs	1 egg yolk
2 oz. butter	2 egg whites
3 anchovies	1 oz. breadcrumbs
2 bread rolls (2½ oz.)	1 oz. butter to garnish

Hard-boil the eggs, cut them in half and take out the yolks. Beat these with the mashed anchovies and rolls, which have been soaked in a little water or milk and then squeezed out. Beat the butter and raw yolk separately and then add to the other ingredients. When the mixture is firm and smooth, add the whisked whites. Grease a baking dish and sprinkle with breadcrumbs. Fill to about a third with the mixture. Decorate with the boiled whites, sprinkle the top with breadcrumbs and butter. Bake in a moderate oven for about 25 minutes. Serve hot with a slice of roll or bread and butter. This makes quite a filling supper.

EGG SALAD

6—8 eggs
6 tablespoons mayonnaise
½ lemon

parsley
salt and pepper

Hard-boil the eggs and then submerge them for a few minutes in cold water so that they are easily shelled. Cut into slices, preferably with a wire cutter. Add a little salt, pepper and lemon juice to the mayonnaise and, if desired, dilute with a little sour cream. Pour the mayonnaise over the sliced eggs. Do not mix or the eggs might break. Serve garnished with chopped parsley.

POTATOES FILLED WITH EGGS

8 large potatoes
3 eggs
3 oz. breadcrumbs

2 oz. butter
anchovy paste
parsley

Bake the potatoes in their jackets, then carefully peel, cut the top open and remove the soft potato inside. Hard-boil the eggs, beat the yolks with the butter and a little anchovy paste, add the finely chopped whites and the mashed potato. Fill the jackets with the mixture, place in a greased fireproof dish, sprinkle the surface with fat and bake in the oven. Serve with vegetables or salad.

POTATOES BAKED WITH CHEESE AND EGGS

2 lb. potatoes	6 eggs
2 oz. bacon	1 onion
3 oz. cheese	salt
2 oz. butter	1 cup cream

Boil the potatoes in their skins and then peel and leave to get cold. Hard-boil the eggs and grate the cheese. Fry the onion in the chopped bacon. Cut the potatoes into slices and chop the eggs then place alternate layers of potato, egg, grated cheese and fried onion in a greased dish. Bake for a short while in the oven and then pour over the cream and return to the oven, baking until the surface is crisp. Serve with vegetable salad.

In Czechoslovakia we do not confine ourselves merely to boiled vegetables served with butter or sauté in butter but prepare many varieties by thickening the liquid with a roux, cream or even eggs. This is particularly the custom in the countryside. Vegetables prepared in this way are filling and if served with potatoes, dumplings or paste often form a meatless meal in themselves.

The commonest vegetable in Czechoslovakia is white cabbage. It is served hot in various ways as an accompaniment to the traditional roast pork or goose. In Bohemia cabbage is stewed in lard or dripping and only lightly dredged with flour while in Moravia it is cooked with a roux, and potatoes or apples are added. In Slovakia cabbage is made with tomatoes and paprika. Raw cabbage and sauerkraut are also used to prepare salads, soup, stuffed cabbage, etc. Other favourite vegetables are cauliflower, kohlrabi, tomatoes and paprika.

Onion and garlic are often added to dishes (particularly potato dishes) as well as dill, chives, parsley and horse-radish.

Cucumbers are popular for making salads. They are also preserved by pickling or bottling and thus make an appetising accompaniment to dishes throughout the year.

GREEN PEAS WITH HAM

1 lb. peas	1 lump sugar
3 oz. ham	1 teaspoon flour
½ pint meat stock	1 teaspoon chopped parsley
1 oz. butter	salt and pepper

Shell the peas, cover with salted water and cook till nearly tender. Fry the chopped parsley in the melted butter, add the finely chopped ham and peas (without water). Gently fry for a few minutes, then dredge with the flour and add the stock. Season and serve with potatoes or rice.

CARROTS STEWED WITH PORK

1 lb. pork	1 oz. butter
1 lb. carrots	½ onion
salt	1 teaspoon plain flour for thickening

Wash the meat and boil in salt water to which half an onion has been added. Clean the carrots, cut into small pieces about the size of thick matchsticks, place in a pan with two or three spoonfuls of stock from the meat and simmer till soft. Then dredge with flour, add a little water and simmer for a few minutes. Cut the meat into portions, add to the carrots and again simmer for a while. Serve with potatoes, potato dumplings or potato cakes.

CABBAGE RISSOLES

1 lb. cabbage
2 oz. butter
2 oz. onion
2 oz. mushrooms
3 oz. meat (smoked)
salt, pepper, garlic

3 eggs
2 bread rolls
3 oz. breadcrumbs
1 gill milk
3 oz. lard or dripping

Clean the cabbage and boil in salt water. When soft, drain and chop finely. Stew the mushrooms separately in a little lard or dripping. Cut the rolls into pieces and soak in milk. Place the cabbage in a bowl, add 2 eggs, the finely diced smoked meat, the mushrooms and rolls from which the milk has been squeezed out. Add fried onion and the seasoning. If the mixture is too soft add a few breadcrumbs. Mix well together and then form into small rissoles, dip in beaten egg and breadcrumbs and fry in lard till a light brown on both sides. Serve with boiled or mashed potatoes.

BAKED CAULIFLOWER

1 lb. cauliflower	½ oz. tomato purée
3 oz. butter	1 oz. flour
2 oz. grated cheese	1 gill milk
2 oz. ham	1 cup cauliflower water
3 oz. mushrooms	salt and pepper

Clean the cauliflower and boil in salt water till nearly soft. Drain off the water for later use and divide the cauliflower into fleurettes. Grease and flour a fireproof dish. Place the cauliflower in the dish and sprinkle with chopped ham. Cut the mushrooms into slices and fry in a little fat, then add them to the cauliflower. Make a white sauce from about 1 oz. of fat, 1 oz. of flour and a cup each of milk and water in which the cauliflower has been boiled. Add the tomato purée and pour the sauce over the cauliflower. Sprinkle grated cheese and melted butter on the top and bake in a medium oven for about 20 minutes. Serve with potatoes or just bread or rolls.

TOASTED TOMATO CHEESE

1 oz. flour	4 eggs
1 oz. butter	salt and red pepper
½ pint cream	tomato purée to taste
2 cups grated cheese	slices of bread

Make a golden roux from the fat and flour dilute with the cream. Season with salt and red pepper and add the beaten eggs, purée and grated cheese. Spread on rounds of bread and bake in the oven.

TOMATOES STUFFED WITH MEAT

8—10 large tomatoes	2 oz. rice
5 oz. smoked meat	3 oz. butter
3 oz. pork	1 onion
3 oz. veal	salt, pepper, red pepper

Cook the smoked meat till tender. Cut the veal and pork into small cubes and simmer in butter together with the chopped onion. Wash the tomatoes, cut off the tops and scoop out the insides. Cut the smoked meat into very small pieces and add to the insides of the tomatoes with the rest of the meat and the boiled rice. Season the inside of each tomato with salt, pepper and red pepper, and fill with the meat and rice. Place on a greased baking tin, dot each tomato with a small piece of butter and bake in a moderate oven till soft, adding a little water at intervals. Serve as an hors d'oeuvre or as the main dish with bread.

TOMATOES STUFFED WITH EGGS AND CHEESE

8 large tomatoes	1 oz. emental cheese
8 eggs	parsley
3 oz. butter	salt and pepper

Wash the tomatoes, cut off the tops and scoop out the insides. Season with salt and pepper. Grate the cheese and put a little in each tomato. Place the tomatoes on a greased baking tin and break an egg into each. Again season with salt and garnish with chopped parsley. Cover with a lid and stew in the oven until the eggs set. Serve with bread or rolls.

FRIED CELERIAC

1 lb. celeriac	2 oz. plain flour
2 eggs	1 gill oil for frying
½ lemon	salt
1 gill milk	

Peel the celeriac and cut into thin slices about ¼ inch thick.
Sprinkle a few drops of lemon juice on each slice and season
with salt, cover and leave for 30 minutes to crisp. Meanwhile
beat the eggs into the milk, add salt and the flour, a little at
a time, and work into a thickish batter. Dip each slice of
celeriac into the batter and fry in hot fat. Serve with mashed
potatoes or potato salad. Garnish each slice of fried celeriac
with tartare sauce (see p. 84).

BEANS WITH SOUR CREAM

1½ lb. green peans	¾ pint stock
1 oz. fat	1 gill sour cream
1 oz. flour	1 tablespoon vinegar
½ onion	2 oz. bacon
salt	

Boil the beans in salt water till nearly tender. Fry the finely
chopped onion in fat, dredge with flour and then add the
stock, stirring well. Add the beans and chopped and fried
bacon and simmer for a few minutes. Season with salt and
a little vinegar and before serving add the thick cream. Heat
through but do not boil. Serve with potatoes.

CABBAGE ROLLS

1 cabbage (about 2 lb.)	2 bread rolls
1 lb. minced pork	1 egg
1 onion	2 oz. bacon
2 oz. lard or dripping	salt, pepper, ginger

Soak the rolls in water or wine. Then squeeze out the liquid and mix them with the minced meat. Add an egg and the seasoning, finely chopped onion and bacon. Scald the cabbage with boiling salt water, remove the leaves and lay them out on the table. Lightly beat the thick veins with a wooden mallet. Place a tablespoon of stuffing on each leaf, roll up, secure firmly at the edge and place in a greased fireproof dish. Add a little water or stock and stew in a hot oven. Serve with potatoes.

SWEET CORN WITH BUTTER

4 cobs sweet corn   2 oz. butter

Remove the leaves and whiskers and throw the cobs into
boiling salt water. Cook for 30—60 minutes according to age.
Then arrange on a plate and pour over melted butter. A slice
of lemon may be added to each cob. It may also be served
with butter mixed with tomato purée or with paprika.

MARROW

1 lb. marrow	1 oz. plain flour
3 oz. fat	2 lumps sugar
1 oz. bacon	salt, caraway seeds
3 oz. onion	vinegar to taste

Fry the chopped onion in the fat. Clean the marrow and cut
it into small strips, add to the onion together with a few caraway seeds and salt, and simmer for about 5 minutes. Dredge
with flour and add a little water. Add sugar and vinegar to
taste. The marrow should be sweetish. Finally cut the bacon
into small pieces, fry separately and then add to the marrow.

MARROW IN BATTER

8 oz. marrow	2 oz. plain flour
2 eggs	5 oz. fat for frying
1 gill milk	salt

Peel the marrow, take out the pith and cut into rounds about
two-thirds of an inch thick. Whisk the eggs, salt and flour
to make a thick batter. Dip each slice of marrow in the batter
and fry in hot fat till golden.

BOHEMIAN CABBAGE

1 white cabbage (about 1 lb.)	1 teaspoon caraway seeds
1 onion	salt
3 oz. lard or dripping	2 lumps of sugar
½ teaspoon flour	1 lemon or a little vinegar

Clean the cabbage and grate on a medium grater. Add a little hot water and simmer, without a lid. Then add the fat and finely chopped onion. When the cabbage is soft add a little vinegar or the juice from 1 lemon. Finally, lightly dredge with flour and simmer for a few minutes.

MORAVIAN CABBAGE

1 white cabbage (about 1 lb.)	1 onion
3 oz. fat	4 lumps of sugar
1—2 oz. flour	3 tablespoons vinegar
caraway seeds	salt

Clean the cabbage and grate on a medium grater. Add a little hot water and simmer till soft. Fry the chopped onion in the fat, dredge with flour to make a golden roux and add the cabbage water. Stir well and add to the cabbage. Season with salt, add the sugar and vinegar. Simmer again till the cabbage is mashy. A sour grated apple may also be added. Serve with meat or potato dishes.

WHITE CABBAGE WITH CREAM

8 oz. white cabbage	pinch pepper
salt, vinegar	2 tablespoons oil
2 tablespoons sugar	1 cup sour cream
pinch caraway seeds	

Remove the thick veins from the cabbage and grate finely. Sprinkle with salt, weigh down with a plate and leave to stand. Mix 2 tablespoons vinegar with ½ small cup water, add some salt, sugar and 2 tablespoons oil and mix well. Season with ground caraway seeds, pepper and finely grated apple. Pour the marinade over the cabbage and finally add the thick cream. For those who cannot digest raw cabbage, scald it with boiling water and parboil before mixing with the marinade.

PICKLED GHERKINS

3 quarts water	5 slices horse-radish
3 tablespoons salt	3 green paprikas
6 lb. small gherkins	strand of dill

Thoroughly wash the gherkins, place in an earthenware pot and pour over hot boiled water. Leave to cool, then arrange in a clean pickling bottle, together with the dill, chopped paprikas and slices of horse-radish. Cover with boiling water containing 3 heaped tablespoons salt. Cover immediately and leave in a cool place to ferment. After about 5 weeks the gherkins are ready for use. Serve with meat, chopped into sandwich spreads or for garnishing. Pickled gherkins are also excellent in sauces.

STUFFED PAPRIKAS

8 paprikas	*Sauce:* 5—7 oz. onions
1 lb. minced meat	3 oz. oil
3 oz. rice	1 lb. tomatoes
1 onion	1 gill sour cream
salt, pepper, parsley	1 teaspoon flour

Wash the paprikas and remove the insides. Fill them with the meat and rice stuffing, which is made as follows. Season the meat, add lightly fried onion and chopped parsley. Mix in the half boiled rice. To make the sauce, finely chop the onions, fry lightly in oil or bacon fat and add ripe tomatoes or tomato purée. Simmer for a few minutes, then season with salt, pass through a sieve and thicken with sour cream and flour. Place the stuffed paprikas in this sauce and simmer for 30 minutes.

VEGETABLE PUDDING

1½ lb. vegetables	1 oz. grated cheese
2 oz. fresh mushrooms	1 oz. fat
3 eggs	2 oz. butter
3 oz. ham	1 teaspoon breadcrumbs

Any vegetables may be used. For example, ½ cauliflower, 1 carrot, ½ small cabbage, 2 leeks, chopped parsley, 1 tablespoon green peas. Clean the vegetables and boil in salt water. Use the water later for soup. Fry the mushrooms in a little fat. Cut the vegetables into small cubes, add the beaten egg yolks, chopped ham, grated cheese and mushrooms. Finally fold in the stiffly whisked whites. Place the mixture in a greased and breadcrumbed bowl, cover and stand in a pot of boiling water. The water must come up to one-third of the bowl. Boil for 1 hour. Carefully turn out and serve hot with melted butter. It may be served with various sauces: lemon, mushroom, chive, or with mayonnaise.

TOMATO SALAD

1 lb. tomatoes	1 onion
2 tablespoons oil	salt and pepper
vinegar and sugar to taste	

Cut the tomatoes into slices, place in a bowl and pour over a little oil and vinegar. Season with salt and sugar and garnish with finely chopped onion or onion rings. Do not add water as the tomatoes themselves contain enough. Serve immediately.

CUCUMBER SALAD

1 large cucumber	1 tablespoon vinegar
salt	sugar to taste
pinch pepper	dill or garlic
3 tablespoons oil	

Peel the cucumber, slice and pour on marinade made as follows. Mix the oil and 1 tablespoon vinegar or lemon juice. Season with salt and sweeten. Add a chopped garlic clove or finely chopped dill. Mix well together. A cup of thick sour cream may be used instead of the oil.

LETTUCE SALAD WITH BACON
(MORAVIAN STYLE)

2 lettuces	1 oz. bacon
salt	vinegar and sugar to taste
1 egg	

Wash the lettuces, place in a bowl and pour on the marinade made from a little vinegar diluted with water, salt and sugar. Hard-boil the egg and when cold cut into slices. Dice the bacon and fry lightly. Serve the salad garnished with the slices of egg and the warm bacon (the latter should not be hot or the lettuce will go limp).

RAW CELERIAC SALAD

8 oz. celeriac	4 tablespoons mayonnaise
1 onion	salt
½ lemon	pepper

Peel the celeriac and grate finely, sprinkle with the lemon juice and mix with the mayonnaise. Garnish with chopped onion.

BEETROOT SALAD

1 lb. beetroot	2 oz. sugar
3 oz. horse-radish	salt
½ teaspoon fennel	2 tablespoons oil
vinegar to taste	

Wash the beetroot and boil in water till soft. Peel and cut into thin slices. Dilute about ½ pint vinegar with water, add salt and the oil. Place beetroot in a bowl, sprinkle with grated horse-radish and fennel and pour on the diluted vinegar. Beetroot salad is usually served with boiled beef or smoked meat.

COOKED CELERIAC SALAD

1½ lb. celeriac	1 onion
2 lumps sugar	vinegar
2 tablespoons oil	salt, pepper

Wash and peel the celeriac and cut into slices. Mix about 3 tablespoons vinegar and a little salt with ½ pint water and cook the celeriac in this for about 20 minutes. Pour into a bowl and add finely chopped onion and about 3 tablespoons oil. Leave for 24 hours. The liquid sets and can be eaten with the celeriac.

CELERIAC SALAD WITH FRUIT

7 oz. celeriac   2 oz. walnuts
2 apples   4 tablespoons mayonnaise
2 bananas

Was and peel the celeriac and cut into small cubes. Cook with a little water and vinegar till soft. Chop the nuts into small pieces. Mix all together with the mayonnaise, sliced bananas and diced apples.

COOKED CARROT SALAD

1 lb. carrots   1 teaspoon sugar
1 gill water and vinegar   parsley, onion
2 tablespoons oil   salt

Wash and scrape the carrots and cook till nearly soft. Add the sugar and oil to the water and vinegar or a little lemon juice and pour this marinade over the carrots. Garnish with chopped onion and parsley. This salad may be combined with peas, cooked cauliflower, asparagus or other vegetables.

CARROT AND APPLE SALAD

8 oz. carrots   2 oz. sugar
7 oz. apples   2 lemons

Wash and scrape the carrots and grate finely. Add the lemon juice and a little grated lemon rind. Sweeten and finally add the grated apple.

MUSHROOMS

Mushrooms are useful for brightening up summer food. They grow abundantly in the woods and forests throughout Czechoslovakia and hundreds of different kinds are to be found. The favourite ones, of course, are the edible boletus which can also be dried or preserved in other ways. Mushrooms improve the taste of soups and sauces and are also used with meat and in stuffings for vegetables, potato doughs, in baked dishes, etc. Favourite suppers are mushroom stew, mushrooms and eggs, fried boletus, mushrooms in cream sauce. They are also excellent as a salad or, boiled in a vinegar solution, as an accompaniment to meat.

MUSHROOMS STEWED WITH ONIONS

1 lb. mushrooms	2 oz. butter
1 oz. onion	caraway seeds, salt

Clean and slice the mushrooms. Fry the finely chopped onion in the butter and when it starts to brown add the mushrooms, a little salt and a few caraway seeds. Stew for 15 minutes. Serve with potatoes or bread.

MUSHROOMS WITH CREAM SAUCE

1 lb. mushrooms	1 oz. onion
1½ oz. butter	1 oz. flour
1 cup sour cream	salt, caraway seeds

Wash the mushrooms and cut into slices. Fry the onion in the butter, add the mushrooms, a little salt and a few caraway seeds. Simmer for 10—15 minutes. Then add the cream mixed with the flour. Cook for a few minutes longer and then serve with potatoes.

MUSHROOMS AND NOODLES
(HALUSHKY)

8 oz. short noodles	2 eggs
2 oz. fat	onion, parsley
12 oz. mushrooms	1 cup milk

Boil the noodles in salted water for 10 minutes till soft. Fry the onion in the fat, add the chopped parsley and mushrooms and stew. Drain the noodles, mix them with the mushrooms and pile the mixture into a greased pie-dish. Bake for a few minutes and then pour over a cup of milk with the beaten eggs. Return to the oven and bake till golden brown. Serve with stewed vegetables or salad.

BAKED POTATOES AND MUSHROOMS

2 lb. potatoes
2 egg yolks
1 gill milk
1 lb. fresh mushrooms

3 oz. fat
1 onion
2 pinches caraway seeds
salt

Clean and slice the mushrooms and simmer with the caraway seeds and a little water for about 20 minutes. Cut the cold cooked potatoes into slices. Grease a fireproof dish and place in a layer of potatoes, sprinkle with mushrooms and fat and then another layer of potatoes. Continue in this way until the dish is full, a layer of potatoes being at the top. Sprinkle the top with melted fat and heat through in the oven. Then pour over the milk in which the yolks have been beaten. The surface may also be sprinkled with grated cheese. Return to the oven to brown.

MUSHROOM SALAD

1 lb. mushrooms
1 gill water
vinegar to taste
allspice

sugar to taste
1 onion
1 bay leaf

Clean and slice the mushrooms and cook them in salted water till nearly soft. Boil a cup of water and a little vinegar separately, then add the seasoning and finely chopped onion. Drain the mushrooms, add to the vinegar water and bring to the boil. Carrot, celeriac, cauliflower and other vegetables may be added to the salad but these should be cut into small pieces and cooked separately to prevent them absorbing the strong mushroom aroma. The salad should have a slight sweet-sour taste.

MUSHROOM GOULASH

1 lb. mushrooms	pinch of sweet red pepper
2 tomatoes	3 oz. onion
4 green paprikas	1½ oz. lard or dripping
salt	

Fry the finely chopped onion in the fat and add the red pepper and cleaned and chopped mushrooms. Cut the green paprikas into rings and the tomatoes into slices and add to the mushrooms. Stew for about 15 minutes. Slices of braised or boiled meat may also be added. As little water as possible should be added to the mushrooms when stewing.

MUSHROOMS WITH EGGS

1 lb. mushrooms	4 eggs
1 oz. butter	salt

Wash the mushrooms and cut them into slices. Place these in hot butter and fry gently until all the water has evaporated. Then add salt and beaten eggs. Stir until the mixture begins to thicken. Serve with toast.

MUSHROOM PUDDING

3 eggs	1 cup milk
3 bread rolls	8 oz. mushrooms
2 oz. semolina	3 oz. butter
salt	parsley

Beat the eggs into the milk, add the semolina, salt and slices of rolls and leave for about 1 hour. Then add the chopped and stewed mushrooms and chopped parsley. Melt the butter in a baking dish, pile in the mixture and bake slowly for 30 minutes. Cut into squares and serve with lettuce salad or stewed vegetables (spinach, peas, etc.).

SANDWICH SPREADS

In recent years it has become more usual to serve open sandwiches with various kinds of spreads rather than to decorate them with bits and pieces of meat, fish and vegetables. Spreads have the advantage that less exciting foods can be combined with more interesting fare and odds and ends of boiled and roast meat and vegetables can also be used up. Spreads served with bread or rolls or as a sandwich filling make a quick and excellent supper, mid-morning snack for the office or school or for picnics.

Fat does not always form the basis of spreads. If less fat has to be used for some reason (for children, people on a diet or old folks) part of it can be replaced by a milk and flour mixture or by a soft cream cheese, whisked cottage cheese or a thick white sauce.

Nutritious spreads containing meat, cheese, eggs, cottage cheese and vegetables are suitable for children while the more piquant varieties with pickled cucumbers, capers or onion are served to adults and guests as an accompaniment to tea or wine.

The Czech housewife serves spreads not only with white bread but also with real rye bread or whole-meal bread.

BEEF SPREAD

8 oz. beef
½ celeriac
1 carrot
1 small onion
salt, lemon rind, bay leaf,
    thyme, ginger

2 bread rolls (2½ oz.)
1 garlic clove
2 eggs
2 oz. dripping

Cut the beef into small pieces and stew in the dripping together with the celeriac and carrot. Add the seasoning and a whole onion. Simmer till the meat is tender, adding a little water if necessary so that about half a cup of juice remains. Soak the rolls in a little water and then squeeze out. Mince the meat, vegetables and rolls finely. Add the garlic crushed with the salt, the eggs and, if the mixture is very thick, a little of the meat juice or, if thin, a few breadcrumbs. Steam the mixture in a greased pudding bowl for 1 hour. When cold spread on bread.

LIVER SPREAD

1 lb. liver (pig's or goat's)
6 small cooked potatoes
2 eggs
1 onion

2 anchovies
3 oz. butter
salt, pepper, mace, lemon rind
garlic clove

Mince the liver, potatoes and onion, add the seasoning, eggs and a little flour or breadcrumbs to thicken. Pile into a pudding bowl and steam for 45 minutes. Then beat the butter and boned anchovies and gradually add to the cold pâté. Spread on black bread and garnish with pickled cucumber.

SALAMI SPREAD

7 oz. soft salami
2 oz. butter
1 teaspoon chopped onion

1 pickled cucumber
anchovy or anchovy paste
bread or bread rolls

Mince the salami and beat with the butter. Add the finely chopped onion, cucumber and anchovy. Spread on rolls or bread.

• SARDINE SPREAD

1 tin sardines
4 oz. butter
2 oz. emental cheese
sweet red pepper

salt
1 onion
lemon juice

Cream the butter and add the grated cheese and sardines. Beat lightly and then add the fish oil, a little salt and red pepper, the finely chopped onion and a few drops of lemon juice.

ROQUEFORT CREAM

3 oz. roquefort cheese   7 oz. butter

Press the cheese through a sieve and beat with the creamed
butter till light and creamy. Gervaise or whipped cream may
also be added to the cheese. Serve with white bread or rolls.

OLOMOUC CHEESES WITH BUTTER

7 oz. Olomouc cheeses   2 oz. chopped onion
7 oz. butter   chives

Cream the cheeses, mix with the butter and beat well. Add
the finely chopped onion and chives. Serve with black bread.

EGG SPREAD (WITH SALAMI)

4 eggs   3 oz. butter
3 oz. salami   onion, chives, French mustard, salt

Halve cold, hard-boiled eggs, take out the yolks and beat
them with the butter. Add a little finely chopped onion and
chives, egg whites and salami and season with French mustard
and salt. Spread on slices of bread.

EGG SPREAD (WITH CHEESE)

4 eggs	5 oz. salami
2 oz. butter	2 oz. cheese
2 oz. flour	2 pickled cucumbers, onion, parsley
1 pint milk	

Melt the butter, add the flour and when it starts to turn golden dilute with the milk. Cook for about 10 minutes. When cold add the diced cheese, cucumbers, salami and hard-boiled eggs. Garnish with chopped parsley.

HORSE-RADISH SPREAD

3 oz. butter	small horse-radish
3 oz. smoked tongue or salami	

Scrape the horse-radish and grate finely. Chop the smoked tongue or salami into small pieces and mix with the creamed butter. Finally add the horse-radish. Spread on white bread or rolls.

RADISH AND CHEESE SPREAD

10 oz. radishes	1 tablespoon chopped chives
3 oz. soft cheese	4 oz. butter

Wash the radishes and grate finely. Mix with the creamed butter and cheese and add the chives and a little salt. This spread is particularly suitable for children.

PUDDINGS, CAKES AND BUNS

A foreigner visiting Czechoslovakia for the first time is surprised by the large choice of puddings and cakes for which the Czechs are famous - yeast cakes, rich cakes, sponges and choux and other pastries. Bukhty (filled buns), kolache (flat fruit buns) and filled rolls made from yeast dough are typically Czech cakes. Yeast is obtainable at any dairy or grocers' shop and the Czech cook knows how to prepare many excellent dishes with it. A soft yeast dough is used for bukhty, kolache and babovka (a sponge cake baked in a special mould) and a stiff dough for large Christmas plaits, Easter mazanec and various small rolls. A speciality made from yeast dough are vdolky and doughnuts. Kolache and bukhty have piquant fillings made from poppy-seed, cottage cheese, jam and damson cheese, and in summer are filled with fresh fruit.

Sponge and flaky doughs are also firm favourites. They are used to make many kinds of rich cakes and buns and also rolls, babovka, etc. Each region, bakery or even household has its own speciality.

Another type of dough made in Czechoslovakia is the pernik (a sort of gingerbread), the best being baked in the Pardubice region - but excellent perniks are made by the Prague bakeries and also at home. Perniks are glazed or filled with damson cheese or fruit, and for special occasions are iced in different colours.

The beautiful cream cakes are much admired. These are made in different shapes with various fillings and elaborately decorated. Small tea-cakes, such as éclairs, petits fours, slices and fancy pastries, are produced by professionals but the housewife also knows how to make such cakes and serves them on Sundays or to guests.

It is the custom to serve certain kinds of cakes on certain occasions. For instance, a family usually has a good babovka on birthdays, a rich cake with candles on name-days, Christmas plaits at Christmas-time, mazanec at Easter and hot cross buns in Lent. At Christmas the housewife also bakes various kinds of biscuits, which used to be decorated with coloured ribbons tied round a fir twig, but nowadays are just attractively arranged on a platter in rows according to the kinds, shape and colour.

On hot summer days light puddings are served - milk puddings with fruit, cold creams, soufflés and ices.

BUKHTY (BUNS WITH FILLING)

1 egg or 2 yolks
1 lb. plain flour
2 oz. sugar
2 oz. butter or margarine
1 oz. baker's yeast

½ pint milk
½ teaspoon salt
vanilla flavouring
lemon rind
3 oz. fat for greasing tin

Poppy-seed filling:
5 oz. ground poppy-seed
3 oz. vanilla sugar
cinnamon

lemon rind
½ pint milk

Mix the yeast and sugar to a paste, add 2 tablespoons flour, 4 tablespoons warm milk, mix to a thick batter and leave in a warm place to sponge. Sieve the rest of the flour, sugar and salt into a bowl, add a little grated lemon rind and vanilla flavouring, 1 whole egg or 2 yolks, the yeast mixture and the rest of the warm milk mixed with the melted butter or margarine. Using a large wooden spoon beat well until the dough is shiny and bubbles form. Cover the bowl with a clean cloth and leave in a warm place to rise. This takes about 45 minutes—1 hour. When it has doubled its size turn onto a floured board and divide into small pieces. Pat out each piece with a floured hand and place a little filling or fruit in the centre of each, press the edges of the dough together and round off the bukhty in the hands. Place on a greased tin, not too close together as they rise during baking, and grease well in between each piece. Leave for 30 minutes to prove and then put into a well-heated oven. After about 10 minutes reduce the heat and bake till golden. The bukhty take about 45 minutes to bake. Then turn them out onto a board and while still hot sprinkle with vanilla sugar and separate them. The above amounts make about 30 small or 25 large bukhty. For poppy-seed filling simmer the poppy-seeds with the milk until a thick mixture is obtained. Sweeten and add a little cinnamon and grated lemon rind. Fill the bukhty with the cold mixture.

Bukhty may also be filled with cottage cheese filling (see p. 153), cherries, plums, apple purée, damson cheese or jam.

LARGE KOLACH

2 eggs
1 lb. plain flour
1 oz. castor sugar
2 oz. butter or margarine
½ oz. baker's yeast
½ pint milk
pinch salt
lemon rind
vanilla flavouring

Topping: 2 oz. butter
3 oz. flour
2 oz. sugar
stoned fruit or damson
   cheese or poppy-
   seed or cottage
   cheese to decorate

Mix the yeast with a spoonful of sugar and flour, add 2 table-spoons warm milk and leave to sponge. Sieve the flour, sugar and salt into a bowl, add the yolks beaten in the rest of the milk, a little grated lemon rind and the vanilla flavouring. Work into a softish dough. Leave for about 30 minutes to rise and then turn onto a greased baking tin, spreading the dough over the tin with wet hands, so that it is about half an inch thick. Decorate with stoned fruit—apricots, plums or sliced apples—or spread with damson cheese or a poppy-seed or cottage cheese filling (see pp. 150, 153). Brush the edges of the kolach with egg.

Before baking sprinkle the kolach with the following topping: crumble the fresh butter into the flour and sugar so that the mixture resembles fine breadcrumbs. The sugar, fat and flour form a sweet layer over the kolach and give it an attractive appearance.

Bake in a well-heated oven for about 30 minutes. When cold cut into squares, rectangles or narrow slices.

COUNTRY-WAKE KOLACHE

3—4 egg yolks
1 lb. plain flour
4 oz. sugar
5 oz. fat
1 oz. baker's yeast

½ teaspoon salt
½ pint milk
2 tablespoons rum
lemon rind
vanilla flavouring

Apple Filling:
1 lb. apples
5 oz. sugar
1 lemon

pinch cinnamon
1 teaspoon rum (optional)
breadcrumbs

Mix the yeast and sugar in a large bowl, add 2 tablespoons flour and 3 tablespoons warm milk, cover and leave for 10 minutes to sponge. Add the rest of the sugar, flour and liquid in which the eggs and salt have been beaten. Work the dough until it is shiny and smooth and leaves the sides of the bowl. Sprinkle lightly with flour, cover with a cloth and leave in a warm place to rise. The dough should not rise too quickly. If a very light and flaky dough is required it should be turned over once or twice during the rising period. The dough is ready when it has risen to one and a half times its original size. If pressed lightly with the fingertip it should rise again immediately and retain no impression. Divide the dough into small pieces, about 1—2 oz. in weight, roll into little balls and place on a greased tin.

For the filling wash, peel and core the apples, and simmer with a little water till soft. Pass through a sieve, add the sugar, a little lemon rind and juice, a pinch of cinnamon and if desired 1 teaspoon rum. If necessary, thicken with a few breadcrumbs. Poppy-seed or cottage cheese filling may be used instead (see pp. 150, 153).

Using the fingers of both hands pat out the middle of each kolach and place a little filling on each. Brush the edges of each kolach with beaten egg. Bake in a moderate oven for 20—30 minutes depending on the size.

FLAKY KOLACHE

3 eggs	8 oz. margarine or butter
1 lb. plain flour	⅔ oz. baker's yeast
1 gill milk	4 tablespoons milk
1 oz. sugar	salt

Mix the fat with about 3 oz. flour and leave in a cool place. Mix the yeast with 4 tablespoons milk and pour this into the rest of the flour and sugar. Add the eggs and work the mixture into a soft dough. Leave for about 1 hour in a warm place to rise. Then roll it out and place on it the rolled out fat. Fold over the edges like an envelope, press together and fold in half. Lightly roll out, fold into three, turn and fold into three again. Leave for 1 hour and then repeat the rolling and folding. Leave for about 15 minutes and then roll out to about ½ inch and cut into squares. Place some thick poppy-seed, apple or nut filling on each square and fold up the corners to the centre, pressing them well together to prevent them opening up during baking. Brush the tops with beaten egg and bake in a hot oven.

Poppy-seed filling:	5 oz. poppy-seed	1 oz. fat
	½ pint milk	lemon rind
	3 oz. sugar	pinch cinnamon
	vanilla essence	chocolate, honey,
		jam (optional)

Grind the poppy-seed and simmer with the milk till soft. If necessary, add a little water from time to time. Add the sugar and simmer for a little longer, stirring all the time. Season with grated lemon rind, vanilla essence and a pinch of cinnamon. A little grated chocolate, a tablespoon of honey or jam may also be added. The filling should be thick but not dry.

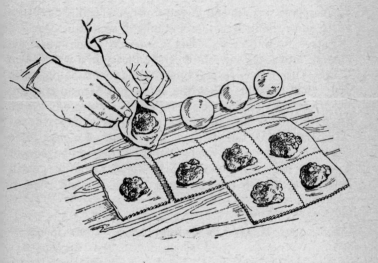

DOMAZHLICE KOLACHE

2 egg yolks
1 lb. plain flour
3 oz. sugar
3 oz. margarine or butter
salt

1 oz. baker's yeast
½ pint milk
lemon rind or vanilla sugar or
   vanilla essence

Mix the yeast and a little sugar with 2 tablespoons flour and
4 tablespoons of milk and leave to sponge. Then add the rest
of the sugar, flour, warm fat and milk in which the eggs and
salt have been beaten. Using a wooden spoon work the
mixture into a soft smooth dough and leave in a warm place
to rise. Turn it over several times during the rising period so
that it will be light. When the dough has risen to one and
a half times its original size turn it onto a board and divide
into four or five large pieces. Form each piece into a round
kolach, patting out the middle so that the edge is higher. Place
different fillings on the kolach, either a different one to each
quarter or rings of different fillings, working from the centre
to the edge. Brush the edge with beaten egg and bake in
a hottish oven for 40—50 minutes.

Damson cheese filling: 5 oz. damson cheese   1 tablespoon
                         2—3 oz. sugar   rum
                                                cinnamon or
                                                lemon rind

Dilute the thick damson cheese with a little water, add the
sugar, pinch cinnamon, a little vanilla essence and grated
lemon or orange rind.

Cottage cheese filling: 1 lb. cottage cheese   1 oz. sultanas
                    2 oz. butter   2 tablespoons
                    3 oz. sugar   cream or milk
                                          2 eggs

Sieve the cottage cheese and add to the creamed butter and sugar and egg yolks. Flavour with vanilla essence and grated lemon rind, add the sultanas and finally fold in the stiffly beaten egg whites.

EASTER MAZANEC

3 egg yolks $\frac{1}{8}$ pint milk
1 lb. plain flour $\frac{1}{2}$ teaspoon salt
3 oz. sugar   2 oz. sultanas
4 oz. butter   1 oz. almonds
1 oz. baker's yeast   1 oz. lemon rind
vanilla essence

Mix the yeast with 1 tablespoon sugar, 1 tablespoon flour and 4 tablespoons warm milk and leave to sponge. Sieve the rest of the flour, sugar and salt into a bowl, add the yeast, yolks, melted butter, the rest of the warm milk, grated lemon rind and a little vanilla essence and knead into a stiff dough. Add the sultanas and peeled and chopped almonds. Leave for 2 hours in a warm place to rise. Form into a round loaf and place on well-greased paper on a tin. Brush the surface with beaten egg and leave for another 10 minutes to prove. Cut a cross into the top and place in a well-heated oven. Bake gently for 45 minutes. When cooked sprinkle liberally with vanilla sugar.

CHRISTMAS PLAIT (VANOCHKA)

2 eggs	½ pint milk
1 lb. plain flour	½ teaspoon salt
4 oz. sugar	1 oz. sultanas
4 oz. fat	1 oz. almonds
1 oz. baker's yeast	1 oz. lemon rind
vanilla essence	

Sieve the sugar, flour and salt into a large bowl. Make a well in the centre and crumble in the yeast. Add a little sugar and 4 tablespoons warm milk and work into a thin batter in the centre of the flour. Cover with a cloth and leave the yeast to sponge. Then add the rest of the warm milk in which the yolks have been beaten (the whites are used for brushing the top of the plait). Add the melted fat, vanilla essence and lemon rind. Knead into a stiff, elastic dough. Then add the sultanas and peeled, chopped almonds. Cover the dough and leave in a warm place to rise, turning over the dough once or twice during this period. It takes 1-2 hours to rise. Then divide it into eight equal parts and form each part into a long roll. The bottom of the vanochka is plaited from four rolls, starting from the middle. Place the plait on greased paper on a tin. The next plait is made from three rolls and placed on the first plait. Finally divide the last roll into two thin ones and twist together. Place on the other plaits and tuck the ends well under the vanochka. The vanochka should be held firmly with slithers of wood to prevent the top slipping. Leave to prove for about 15 minutes and then brush with the beaten whites, sprinkle with a few chopped almonds and bake in a well-heated oven for 45 minutes—1 hour. Sprinkle the top with sugar while it is still warm.

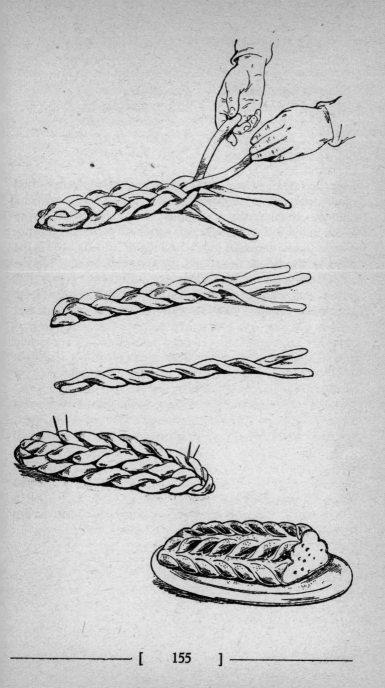

VDOLKY (A KIND OF DOUGHNUT)

1 egg	½ pint milk
1 lb plain flour	1 teaspoon rum
2 oz. sugar	1 oz. fat for brushing top
1 oz fat	7 oz. damson cheese
¾ oz. baker's yeast	3 oz. hard cottage cheese
½ teaspoon salt	1 cup thick sour cream

Beat the fat, sugar and eggs in a bowl, add the sieved flour, salt, spongy yeast (yeast mixed with 1 tablespoon of sugar and flour and 4 tablespoons warm milk) and the rest of the liquid. Work into a soft, smooth dough and leave to rise for 1 hour. Then roll out about 20 pieces, roll each into a ball and again leave to rise. Place the vdolky on a greased tin and bake in a hot oven or on a girdle. When done, brush each with melted butter and damson cheese, sprinkle with grated cottage cheese and cream. Vdolky may also be fried in hot fat.

SALTY YEAST DOUGH FOR ROLLS
OR SALT STICKS

1 egg	1 oz. baker's yeast
1 lb. plain flour	1 gill milk
½ teaspoon sugar	½ teaspoon salt
2 oz. fat	poppy-seeds or caraway seeds

Mix the sugar and yeast and when it begins to soften add
1—2 tablespoons flour and 2—3 tablespoons warm milk.
Leave for 5 minutes to sponge and then add it to the flour,
egg and warm fat. Mix with the rest of the warm milk and
salt until the dough leaves the sides of the bowl. Leave to rise
for 1 hour. Then roll out into long sticks or form into long
plaits. The dough can also be cut into triangles, which are
then brushed with melted fat and rolled up from the broad
side to the tip. Leave to prove and then sprinkle with poppy-
seeds and salt, or caraway seeds and salt, and bake in
a moderate oven.

DOUGHNUTS

4—5 egg yolks	1 oz. baker's yeast
1 lb. plain flour	2 tablespoons rum
1 oz. castor sugar	½ pint milk
3 oz. butter	pinch salt
1 lb. lard for frying	redcurrant jam

Cream the butter and sugar and gradually beat in the egg yolks. Mix the yeast with 1 teaspoon sugar, 2 tablespoons warm milk and 1 tablespoon flour and leave to sponge. Add the flour, risen yeast and the rest of the milk to the yolk mixture and work all together into an elastic dough. Leave for about 45 minutes to rise. Lightly roll out on a floured board and using a cutter or upturned glass cut out rounds about 2 inches in diameter. Place a little redcurrant or apricot jam on half of the rounds and cover with the other half. Press the edges well together and again cut with the cutter or glass to give each doughnut a good shape. Place on a warm floured cloth and cover with another cloth. After about 10 minutes turn them over and leave for another 10 minutes to rise again. Melt the lard in a deep pan (the fat should be at least 2 inches deep). When it is very hot place in three or four doughnuts and cover. The steam helps the dough to rise well. After 2 minutes take off the cover and turn over the doughnuts. When they are golden on both sides take them out and place on a rack or blotting paper to drain. Sprinkle immediately with sugar. In Czechoslovakia doughnuts are made principally for country wakes and in the winter months. Serve with white coffee.

CELESTIAL FAVOURS

1 egg	2 tablespoons rum
2 egg yolks	pinch salt
8 oz. plain flour	lemon rind
½ oz. butter	5 oz. lard for frying
2 tablespoons sugar	

Sieve the flour, sugar and salt onto a board, crumble in the butter and add the beaten eggs, rum and a little grated lemon rind. Work into an elastic dough. Roll out thinly, cut into squares or use a cutter to make different sized stars. Place in hot lard and fry quickly on both sides. Dust with vanilla sugar.

POPPY-SEED ROLL

1 lb. plain flour	¾ oz. baker's yeast
2 eggs	4 tablespoons milk
2 oz. sugar	pinch salt
8 oz. butter or margarine	

Work about 3 oz. flour into the fat and leave in a cool place. Sieve the rest of the flour into a bowl and mix with the yeast which has been put to sponge with the warm milk, a little sugar and 1 tablespoon flour. Add the salt and yolks to the flour and work into an elastic dough. Leave in a warm place to rise. Then roll out, place the fat in the middle, fold the edges like an envelope and press well together and fold the whole in half. Lightly roll out and fold into three, turn and again fold. Leave for 1 hour and then roll out to ½ inch thick, strew with poppy-seed filling, roll up firmly, press the edge to the roll and place on a greased tin. Brush with beaten white and bake in a well-heated oven for about 45 minutes. Then cut into slices.

SWISS ROLL

4 eggs	1 oz. butter
3 oz. sugar	jam for filling
3 oz. plain flour	

Pour 1 tablespoon boiling water onto the yolks and whisk well. Add two-thirds of the sugar to the yolks and whisk to a thick cream. Whisk the egg whites separately and fold in the rest of the sugar. Add spoonfuls of flour to the yolks and finally fold in the stiffly whisked whites. Pour onto well greased paper in a baking tin and bake in a hot oven. If the paper is well greased the roll can easily be removed. If it is to be filled, wrap it up in a damp towel while still hot; when cold, unroll and spread with jam, coffee or chocolate cream and then roll up again. Coffee or chocolate icing may be spread over the top of the roll.

SPONGE BABOVKA

6 eggs	vanilla essence, lemon rind
8 oz. sugar	1 oz. almonds
7 oz. plain flour	1 oz. butter

Beat the eggs and sugar in a bowl standing in hot water until the mixture thickens. Remove from the fire and stir until it cools. Then add the flour, a spoonful at a time. Grease a babovka mould with melted butter and when it hardens sprinkle with flour. Pile in the sponge so that the mould is two-thirds full and bake in a slowish oven for 30—40 minutes. Turn out onto a rack. Vanilla essence, lemon rind, chopped almonds or sultanas may be added to the dough, or half the dough may be coloured brown with cocoa and then layers of white and brown mixture piled into the mould.

SPONGE OMELETTE

4 eggs	1 oz. butter
3 oz. sugar	jam
3 oz. plain flour	

Pour 1 tablespoon of boiling water onto the yolks and whisk. Add two-thirds of the sugar and continue whisking until the mixture is like thick cream. Whisk the whites and lightly fold in the rest of the sugar. Add the flour, a spoonful at a time, to the yolks and finally fold in the stiffly whisked whites. Spread on a greased and floured tin and bake in a moderate oven for 7 to 10 minutes. Spread with a sharp jam and fold in half.

CHILDREN'S SPONGE FINGERS

3 eggs	3 oz. plain flour
3 oz. sugar	1 oz. butter

Whisk the yolks with two-thirds of the sugar. Whisk the whites and fold in the rest of the sugar. Add the whites to the yolks and lightly fold in the flour. Using a piping bag with a round nozzle squirt fingers onto a greased and floured tin. Leave for a few minutes to dry and then sprinkle with castor sugar. Again leave for a few minutes for the sugar to soak in and then bake in a moderate oven. Use a palette knife to remove them from the tin. These sponge fingers can be used for making trifles or as an accompaniment to fruit purées or custard.

INDIANKY

3 egg yolks	*Filling:* 1 pint whipped cream
4 egg whites	2 tablespoons icing sugar
3 oz. plain flour	*Icing:* 3 oz. fat
2 oz. castor sugar	3 oz. icing sugar
1 oz. butter	½ oz. cocoa
	1 tablespoon milk
	1 tablespoon cornflour

Stiffly whisk the egg whites and fold in about 1 oz. sugar. Beat the yolks, add the rest of the sugar and the flour and gradually add to the whites. Grease and flour a baking tin and pipe on blobs of sponge. Bake in a hot oven. Cut the sponges in half, place the bottoms in paper cups, pile on the whipped cream beaten together with the icing sugar, cover with the top halves and decorate with the icing. To make the icing mix the cornflour and milk over a low flame until it thickens, then add the creamed fat and sugar, and cocoa.

MARBLE BABOVKA

8 oz. plain flour	3 eggs
6 oz. sugar	1 gill milk
4 oz. fat	lemon rind
3 tablespoons cocoa	vanilla essence

Cream the fat, add the sugar and then egg yolks, one after another. Beat into a thick cream. Alternately add the milk and flour. Stiffly whisk the egg whites and fold in a little sugar. Add to the yolks. Divide the dough into two parts and lightly fold in the sieved cocoa into one half. Grease a babovka mould and pile in alternate layers of light and dark dough. Bake in a moderate oven for about 45 minutes, then carefully turn out and sprinkle immediately with sugar.

COTTAGE CHEESE KOLACH

3 oz. soft cottage cheese
3 oz. sugar
3 oz. roasted walnuts
3 eggs
1—2 oz. breadcrumbs
3 oz. fat
jam, nuts, grated chocolate to decorate

Cream the fat and sugar and add the egg yolks. Mix in the sieved cottage cheese and chopped nuts. Stiffly whisk the whites and fold into the dough alternately with the breadcrumbs. Pile into a well-greased cake tin and bake in a moderate oven. Spread a little jam on the finished kolach and decorate with grated nuts and chocolate.

RICH BABOVKA

4 eggs
1 lb. plain flour
7 oz. castor sugar
7 oz. butter
½ pint milk
½ oz. baking powder
2 tablespoons rum
lemon rind
vanilla sugar

Cream the fat and sugar and gradually add the yolks, one at a time. Beat a little longer and then add alternately the sieved flour and baking powder and the milk. Finally fold in the stiffly whisked whites. Grease a mould with melted fat, sprinkle with breadcrumbs and pile in the dough. Bake in a moderate oven for 30—45 minutes. If a skewer or metal knitting needle is inserted into the finished cake it should come out cleanly, without any dough clinging to it. Turn the babovka onto a rack and sprinkle liberally with vanilla sugar while still hot.

BABOVKA WITH NUTS AND CHOCOLATE

6 eggs	½ oz. baking powder
1 lb. plain flour	6 oz. chopped nuts
8 oz. sugar	3 tablespoons rum
8 oz. butter	5 oz. grated chocolate or cocoa
½ pint milk	

Cream the butter and sugar and gradually add the egg yolks. Mix in the flour and baking powder, finely chopped nuts and milk with rum. Finally fold in the stiffly whisked egg whites. Divide the dough into two parts, and add the grated chocolate or cocoa to one of them. Grease a mould and sprinkle with fine breadcrumbs or finely crumbled sponge. Pile in layers of light and dark dough and bake in a moderate oven for 40—50 minutes.

APPLE KOLACH

4 eggs	½ teaspoon baking powder
6 oz. flour	4 tablespoons milk
7 oz. sugar	3 tablespoons cornflour
3 oz. fat	1 lb. apples
1 oz. butter	vanilla sugar

Cream the fat and sugar and gradually add the egg yolks. Beat until light and creamy. Then add alternately the cold milk and sieved flour, cornflour and baking powder. Finally fold in the stiffly whisked egg whites. Place the dough in a well-greased and breadcrumbed baking tin, cover with a layer of thinly sliced apples and sprinkle with melted butter. Bake in a moderate oven for about 30 minutes. Sprinkle with vanilla sugar when done.

RICH POTATO SLICES

7 oz. sugar	vanilla essence
2 eggs	½ lemon
1 oz. flour	pinch baking powder
7 oz. potatoes	¼ pint whipped cream
3 oz. walnuts	

Beat the egg yolks and sugar till light and creamy. Add the finely chopped nuts and cold, cooked and finely grated potatoes. Add the grated lemon rind, flour, a little vanilla essence and baking powder. Mix well together and fold in the stiffly whisked egg whites. Bake on a greased tin in a moderate oven till golden. Leave to cool and then spread with whipped cream or a butter cream, or cut in half, spread with jam and decorate with a chocolate icing.

BUBLANINA (FRUIT BUBBLE CAKE)

8 oz. plain flour	2 lb. fruit
5—6 oz. sugar	lemon rind
4 oz. fat	vanilla essence
3 eggs	vanilla sugar
¼ pint milk	

Warm the fat slightly and then cream with the sugar. Add the egg yolks and continue beating until the mixture is thick and creamy. Add spoonfuls of flour and milk alternately with a little grated lemon rind and vanilla essence. Fold in the stiffly whisked egg whites. Pile into a baking tin so that the layer is about 1 inch thick. Dot with washed and stoned fruit (cherries are the most suitable). Bake in a slowish oven till the surface is a light golden colour. Before serving sprinkle with vanilla sugar.

QUICK CRUMBLE KOLACH

1 egg
8 oz. plain flour
3 oz. sugar
3 oz. butter or margarine
½ teaspoon baking powder
vanilla essence
lemon rind

Filling: 3 apples
2 oz. sugar
1 oz. butter or margarine

Sieve the flour, sugar and baking powder onto a board. Crumble in the fat with the fingertips. Make a well in the middle and break in the egg. Add a little vanilla essence and grated lemon rind. Knead the dough and then crumble it. Place half of the crumble into a well greased and floured tin. Add a layer of peeled and finely chopped apples, sprinkle with sugar and melted butter and cover with the rest of the crumble. Sprinkle the surface with fat and sugar. Bake in a moderate oven till golden.

COTTAGE CHEESE SLICES

Pastry base: 8 oz. plain flour
3 oz. sugar
6 oz. sugar
2 oz. butter
2 egg yolks
lemon rind

Filling: 2 lb. soft cottage
cheese
3 oz. sugar
2 eggs
2 oz. sultanas
vanilla essence

Sponge top: 4 eggs
3 oz. sugar
3 oz. flour

Sieve the flour and sugar onto a board, crumble in the fat, add a little grated lemon rind and bind with the yolks. Roll out into a thin layer and place on a greased tin. For the filling, sieve the cottage cheese, beat with the sugar and egg yolks, add a little vanilla essence, sultanas and stiffly whisked egg whites. Spread on the pastry. For the sponge, beat the yolks and sugar till creamy, fold in the stiffly whisked whites and flour alternately. Place on top of the cottage cheese filling and bake in a moderate oven for 40 minutes.

RASPBERRY MERINGUE KOLACH

7 oz. plain flour
3 oz. castor sugar
3 oz. butter
2 egg yolks
3—4 egg whites

1—2 tablespoons milk
pinch baking powder
3 tablespoons raspberry jam
1 lemon
2 oz. sugar for meringue

Sieve the flour, sugar and baking powder onto a board and add the grated lemon rind. Crumble in the fat and bind with the egg yolks and a little milk. Mix the dough well and roll out into a round; place this in a greased bake tin. Bake for about 30 minutes and when it starts to turn golden leave to cool. Stiffly whisk the whites, fold in the sugar and finally the jam. Pile on top of the kolach and place in a very slow oven till the meringue dries.

COTTAGE CHEESE KOLACH

8 oz. plain flour
2 oz. castor sugar
4 oz. butter
1 egg
½ teaspoon baking powder
3—4 tablespoons milk
1 egg for brushing top

Filling: 2 eggs
1 lb. soft cottage cheese
3 oz. sugar
1 oz. sultanas
lemon rind
vanilla essence

Sieve the flour, sugar and baking powder onto a board, crumble in the butter, add the egg and a little milk to make a soft dough. Leave in a cool place for 20 minutes and then roll out two equal rectangular sheets. Using a floured rolling-pin transfer one to a baking tin. To make the filling, cream cottage cheese with sugar and egg yolks, add the sultanas, a little vanilla essence, grated lemon rind and stiffly whisked egg whites. Spread mixture over the pastry, then cover with the other piece of dough and press the edges together. Brush with beaten egg and bake in a moderate oven for 25—30 minutes.

LATTICE KOLACH

2 eggs
10 oz. plain flour
3 oz. castor sugar
3 oz. butter or margarine
2 tablespoons milk

pinch baking powder
lemon rind
poppy-seed or cottage cheese,
or jam or damson cheese or
apple for filling
chopped almonds (optional)

Sieve the flour, sugar and baking powder onto a board, with a little grated lemon rind. Rub in the fat and make a well in the centre. Break in 1 egg and add the milk. Work into a dough, using a knife, and then the hands (but not too long, or the fat will get too soft). Divide the dough into two parts. Roll out one and place in a greased baking tin. Spread with poppy-seed or cottage cheese filling, jam, damson cheese or apple filling. Roll out the other half of the dough and either place it on top or cut it into strips and make a lattice. Beat the second egg, brush the top of the kolach and, if desired, sprinkle it with chopped almonds.

KOLACH WITH JELLIED FRUIT

1 egg yolk
8 oz. plain flour
5 oz. butter
2 oz. sugar
lemon rind
2 tablespoons jam

1 lb. fruit (strawberries, redcurrants, apricots etc.)

Jelly: 1 gill water
1 oz. gelatine
3 oz. sugar

Edging: 2½ oz. ground almonds
5 oz. sugar
½ egg white

Sieve the flour and sugar and crumble in the fat. Add the egg yolk and mix into a light pastry. Roll out and place in a greased baking or cake tin. Bake in a hot oven and when cold spread with jam to prevent the jelly soaking in. Cover with a layer of fruit. Mix the beaten egg white with the ground almonds and sugar to a thick mixture, form into a long roll and place round the edge of the kolach. Dissolve the sugar and gelatine in water and spoon onto the top of the fruit. Leave to set and then cut into pieces.

APPLE ROLL (STRUDEL)

Strudel dough: 10 oz. plain flour
1 egg
1 gill warm water
salt
1 oz. butter

2 lb. apples
3 oz. breadcrumbs
3 oz. sugar mixed with
cinnamon
4 oz. fat
1 oz. sultanas

Sieve the flour onto a board and make a well in the middle. Beat the egg into the warm water, add a few grains of salt and the warm butter. Pour this into the flour and using a knife work it into the dough. Then knead the dough with the hands until it is smooth and elastic and does not stick to the board. Sprinkle with a little flour and leave in a warm place (under a warmed pot is best) for about 30 minutes. Divide the dough into two parts. Place a cloth on the board and sprinkle it lightly with flour. Roll out half the dough with a rolling-pin and when it is a fairly thin sheet begin to pull it out carefully with the hands, from the centre to the edge, until it is paper-thin. Sprinkle with melted fat, breadcrumbs and grated apple. Add the sugar, cinnamon and sultanas and again sprinkle with melted fat. Wind up the roll, starting from the wider side, by carefully lifting the cloth and turning the dough over and over. Then roll it onto a greased tin, brush the surface with fat and place in a moderate oven, baking for about 30 minutes. Treat the other half of the dough in the same way. Brush with fat during baking and sprinkle with sugar when it is taken from the oven. Cut into slices when cold.

BAKED APPLE DUMPLINGS

Pastry: 8 oz. fat
8 oz. flour
6 tablespoons water
1 egg yolk
1 tablespoon vinegar or
    lemon juice
pinch salt

1 lb. apples
3 oz. jam
egg to glaze
chopped almonds
    (optional)
vanilla sugar

Sieve the flour and knead about a quarter of it with the fat and leave in a cool place to harden. Make a well in the rest of the flour and pour in the water mixed with a little salt, the vinegar or lemon juice and the beaten egg yolk. First work the liquid into the flour with a knife and then lightly with the hands until the pastry is elastic and does not stick to the board. Leave for a few minutes and then roll out into a square. Place the lump of flour and fat in the middle, fold the corners together like an envelope and roll out and fold three times. Leave for a while in a cool place and repeat twice more. Finally roll out and cut into squares. Place a peeled and cored apple on each square, fill the middle with a little jam, pull up the corners of the dough and press well together. Brush the surface with beaten egg. A few finely chopped almonds may be sprinkled on the top. Place the apple dumplings on a baking tin and bake in a hot oven for a few minutes; then lower the temperature and bake till the apples are done. Before serving sprinkle with vanilla sugar.

VOL-AU-VENT

The pastry for Baked Apple Dumplings (p. 174) is cut into different shapes and small pieces are filled with cranberries or vegetables as an accompaniment to roast meat. The smallest are filled with caviar, creamed cheese etc. Large ones may also be made and filled with a meat mixture. They are then served as an hors d'oeuvre. Cut out rounds and in half of them cut out holes in the middle. Place the full rounds on a greased tin, brush with egg white and cover with the rings. Brush the tops with egg.

COTTAGE CHEESE SCRAMBLE

1 lb. cottage cheese	4 eggs
1 oz. sugar	1 cup milk
few grains salt	1 oz. fat
lemon rind	2 oz. fat for greasing tin
3—4 oz. plain flour mixed with fine semolina	

Cream the butter and sugar. Add the egg yolks and after mixing well add the sieved cottage cheese and milk. Stiffly whisk the whites and add to the mixture alternately with the flour. Turn into a greased frying pan and fry like a thick omelette or place in hot fat in a baking tin and bake in the oven. When the underside is golden, tear it apart with a fork and turn it over. Serve sprinkled with sugar and with fruit juice or compote.

ECLAIRS

4 eggs
5 oz. plain flour
3 oz. fat
½ pint water
few grains salt

Cream filling: 2 egg yolks
4 oz. sugar
7 oz. butter
3 tablespoons black
coffee
vanilla essence

Add the salt and fat to the water and bring to the boil. Throw
in the sieved flour, stirring all the time. Remove immediately
from the stove and stir quickly until the dough is smooth and
shiny. Then again place on the stove and cook gently through.
Finally turn into a cold bowl and continue stirring until the
mixture has cooled. Gradually add one egg after another and
stir in well. When the dough is thick and and shinily smooth,
pile it into a piping bag and pipe onto a tin. Bake in a well-
heated oven. When cold cut in half and fill with coffee
cream, made as follows. Cream the yolks with the sugar, add
a little vanilla essence and strong black coffee. Heat but do
not boil. Pour into a china bowl and leave to cool. Cream the
butter and add to the mixture.

SIMPLE PERNIK (GINGERBREAD)

1 lb. plain flour
5 oz. sugar
10 tablespoons honey
1 egg
2 oz. fat
1 gill milk or black coffee
½ oz. baking powder

Pernik seasoning: ¼ teaspoon each cinnamon, clove, vanilla, aniseed, allspice, badian

Sieve the sugar, baking powder, flour and pernik seasoning into a bowl. Warm the honey and fat, add to the egg milk or black coffee and pour into the flour. Work into a dough and leave for 1—2 hours to stand. If the dough becomes too stiff, put it in a warm place to soften. The seasoning and baking powder work on the flour and make the dough light. Grease a baking tin and sprinkle with flour. Pile in the mixture and brush the top with beaten egg or sweetened milk or coffee. Place in a well-heated oven and after a few minutes reduce the heat. If the pernik is baked too quickly a hard crust forms and the inside remains too soft; if baked too slowly it dries out and is hard. So first bake in a hot oven and reduce the temperature to about 300° F. Keep the pernik in a tin so that it does not dry out. It is best eaten a week or a fornight after baking.

FILLED PERNIK

10 oz. plain wheat or
  rye flour
8 oz. sugar
1 egg
2 tablespoons honey
2 tablespoons milk
1 tablespoon rum
½ tablespoon baking powder

Pernik seasoning: cinnamon
  vanilla
  pinch fennel
  lemon or
    orange rind
Filling: 5 tablespoons damson
  cheese
  1 teaspoon grated
    lemon rind
  8 tablespoons chopped
    walnuts
  4 tablespoons chopped
    dates

Sieve the flour, sugar, baking powder and seasoning onto a board. Warm the honey, add the rum, milk and beaten egg and stir into the flour. Work into a stiffish dough. If it is too soft add a little more flour. Roll out strips 2 inches thick. Place the filling in the middle and press the long sides of the strips well together, as illustrated opposite. Place the dough joined side downwards on a greased tin, brush the top with beaten egg and bake in a moderate oven for about 30 minutes. The above ingredients make 3 to 4 rolls. When cold cut the rolls into oblique slices. The pernik remains moist for a long time. The filling is made from finely chopped fruit and nuts, mixed with damson cheese.

HONEY PERNIK

3 eggs
1 lb. plain flour
1 pint honey
½ teaspon bicarbonate of soda

4 oz. butter
2 oz. nuts
2 oz. almonds
vanilla, ground cloves,
    lemon rind

Warm the honey till it is liquid, melt the butter in it and add the egg yolks, stirring all the time. Pour into the sieved dry ingredients. Beat the dough well and then fold in the stiffly whisked whites. Grease a baking tin and sprinkle with flour. Carefully pour in the dough, sprinkle the top with chopped nuts and bake in a moderate oven for about 30 minutes, until the pernik remains firm to the touch. When cold, cut into slices or squares.

ICED PERNIK

2 eggs
1 lb. plain flour
8 oz. sugar
1 tablespoon rum
2 tablespoons honey

½ teaspoon bicarbonate of soda
lemon rind
Pernik seasoning: ¼ teaspoon each cinnamon, clove, vanilla, aniseed, allspice, badian

Sieve the flour, add the sugar, bicarbonate of soda and seasoning. Warm the honey and mix with the beaten eggs and rum. Pour into the flour and work all together into a stiff dough. Leave to stand overnight. The next day roll out a thick layer and cut out figures or various shapes. Brush with egg and bake in a hot oven. Ice when cold with lemon or rum icing.

LEMON ICING

8 oz. icing sugar
2 tablespoons lemon juice
2—3 tablespoons boiling water

Sieve the icing sugar and add the lemon juice and boiling water. Beat in a china bowl until the icing thickens and whitens. If it is too thin add sugar, if too thick dilute with a little water.

RUM ICING

8 oz. sugar
3 tablespoons rum
2 tablespoons boiling water

Proceed in the same way as for Lemon Icing (above).

FRUIT DUMPLINGS MADE WITH COTTAGE CHEESE

8 oz. mixed flour and fine semolina
1 egg
1 oz. fat
3 oz. cottage cheese
1 gill milk
salt

Garnish: 2 oz. butter
2 oz. hard cottage cheese
1 oz. sugar

If hard cottage cheese is used, it should be grated; soft cottage cheese is beaten with the fat, salt and egg. Add alternately the flour and milk and mix until a soft elastic dough is formed. Turn onto a floured board, lightly roll out and cut into squares. Place fruit on the squares, roll up into a ball and throw into boiling water. Cook for 5—8 minutes. Drain and serve sprinkled with sugar and grated, hard cottage cheese (or grated pernik) and melted butter.

FRUIT DUMPLINGS FROM POTATO DOUGH

8 oz. mixed flour and fine
    semolina
1 egg
2 large potatoes
about 8 tablespoons milk
salt
fruit for filling

Garnish: 2 oz. butter
          2 oz. cottage cheese
          1 oz. sugar

Use potatoes cooked the day before. Grate them and mix with the flour and salt. Make a well in the middle and break in the egg and add the milk. Work into a stiff dough. Turn out onto a floured board, roll out fairly thinly and cut into squares. Place fruit in the middle of each square, roll up into a ball and throw into boiling water, slightly salted; cook for 5—7 minutes. Serve sprinkled with sugar, grated cottage cheese and melted butter.

FRUIT DUMPLINGS FROM YEAST DOUGH

1 lb. mixed flour and
    fine semolina
½ pint milk
⅓ oz. baker's yeast
1 egg
1 lb. fruit

1 tablespoon sugar
salt

Garnish: 2 oz. butter
         2 oz. cottage cheese
         2 oz. sugar

Mix the yeast with the sugar and a little warm milk. Leave to sponge and then add to the sieved flour and bind with the rest of the warm milk mixed with the salt and egg. Beat well and then leave for 1 hour in a warm place, sprinkled with flour. Form into a long roll and cut off small pieces. Wrap each piece around fruit (such as plums, apricots etc.) and leave on the board for another 15 minutes to prove. Throw into boiling water and cook for 5 minutes, turn over and cook for another 3—5 minutes. Remove from the water and prick with a fork to let the steam escape. Serve sprinkled with grated cottage cheese or grated pernik, sugar and melted butter.

YEAST PANCAKES

1 egg or 2 yolks	lemon rind
1 oz. sugar	salt
1 pint milk	damson cheese or jam
½ oz. baker's yeast	*Garnish:* 2 oz. butter
8 oz. flour	2 oz. sugar
3 oz. fat	cinnamon

Mix the yeast and sugar, add a little warm milk and 1 table-spoon flour and leave to sponge. Then add the eggs and a pinch of salt, mix well and add alternately the flour and the rest of the warm milk. Beat well to prevent any lumps forming. Leave to rise to double its original size. Then ladle small amounts into a greased pan and fry on both sides till golden. Spread damson cheese or jam on the pancakes or sprinkle with butter and sugar mixed with cinnamon.

PANCAKES

2 eggs	7 oz. plain flour
1½ oz. sugar	2 oz. fat
1 pint milk	7 oz. jam

Whisk the eggs with the sugar and a pinch of salt. Gradually add the flour and milk, whisking all the time to prevent lumps forming. Grease a frying pan and ladle in small amounts of batter at a time. Fry on both sides till golden, spread with jam and roll up.

BAKED PANCAKES WITH COTTAGE CHEESE

1 pint milk
2 eggs
1 oz. sugar
7 oz. flour
lemon rind
Custard: ½ pint milk
    2 lumps sugar
    1 egg

2 oz. fat for frying
1 oz. vanilla sugar
Filling: 1 lb. cottage cheese
    2 eggs
    3 oz. sugar
    2 oz. butter
    1 oz. sultanas

Beat the eggs in a little milk, add the sugar and grated lemon rind and gradually spoon in the flour and the rest of the milk. Ladle into hot fat and fry thin pancakes. Cream the cottage cheese, egg, yolks and sugar, add the butter, sultanas and stiffly whisked egg whites. Spread the filling on the pancakes, roll them up and cut in half. Arrange in fireproof dish and bake for a few minutes in the oven. Then pour over custard—the milk mixed with the beaten egg and sugar. Return to the oven and bake for about 20 minutes. Serve sprinkled with vanilla sugar.

BISCUITS WITH PARMESAN

1 egg yolk
2 oz. fat
5 oz. plain flour
2 oz. Parmesan cheese

1 oz. almonds
½ oz. baker's yeast
1—2 tablespoons milk
sugar

Mix the yeast with a little sugar, warm milk and flour and leave to sponge. Crumble the fat into the flour, sprinkle in the grated Parmesan and a little salt, add the risen yeast and work into a stiffish dough. Leave in a warm place for 30 minutes to rise. Then roll out thinly and cut into various shapes. Brush with egg, sprinkle with chopped almonds and bake in a moderate oven.

BAKED PUDDING

3—4 eggs	7—8 oz. plain flour mixed with
1 oz. sugar	fine semolina
1 pint milk	pinch baking powder
pinch salt	3 oz. fat for greasing tin

Whisk the egg yolks in half the milk, add the sugar and salt. Spoon in the rest of the milk and the flour alternately. The mixture should be fairly thick. Finally fold in the stiffly whisked egg whites. Melt the fat (preferably butter) in a baking tin and when it starts to brown, pour in the pudding mixture. Bake in a hot oven and when the bottom is a light golden, cut into quarters, turn over and finish baking in a cooler oven. Take out of the oven and immediately sprinkle liberally with sugar. Serve with fruit juice, compote or a fruit sauce.

COTTAGE CHEESE BREAD PUDDING

1 lb. white loaf	3 oz. fat
1 lb. soft cottage cheese	5 oz. sugar
1½ pints milk	1 oz. sultanas
2 egg yolks	vanilla essence
lemon rind	

Cream half the fat with the sugar, add a little vanilla essence, grated lemon rind, 1 egg yolk and the soft cottage cheese. Mix well together and if necessary add a little milk. Cut the loaf into slices and moisten with milk. Place a layer in a greased pie-dish, sprinkle with melted fat, spread on some of the cottage cheese and strew with sultanas. Continue making layers of bread and cheese, ending with a layer of bread. Beat the other yolk in a cup of milk and pour over the pudding. Bake in a moderate oven for 30—45 minutes. Serve sprinkled with vanilla sugar.

SWEET RAVIOLI FROM POTATO DOUGH

8 oz. flour mixed with
   fine semolina
2 large cooked potatoes
1 egg
damson cheese

salt
milk
2 oz. butter
2 oz. sugar

Grate the potatoes, mix them with the flour and salt, add the egg and a little milk and work into a dough. Roll out about ¼ inch thick. Cut into squares about 3 inches long. In the middle of each place a little damson cheese or poppy-seed filling, fold in half like a letter and press the edges well together. Throw into boiling water and cook for 5 minutes. Drain and sprinkle with melted butter and sugar mixed with grated pernik or fried breadcrumbs.

RICE SOUFFLE

1½ pints milk
6 oz. sugar
4 oz. butter
7 oz. rice

vanilla essence
3 eggs
3 apples
lemon rind

Boil the milk and add the washed rice, 2 oz. butter and 2 oz. sugar. Simmer until the rice is soft, stirring from time to time. Leave to cool. Beat the egg yolks with 3 oz. sugar, add the grated lemon rind, a little vanilla essence and cold rice. Fold in the stiffly whisked egg whites. Grease a pie-dish with remaining butter, pile in half the pudding, place on a layer of sliced apples, sprinkle with remaining sugar and then cover with the rest of the pudding. Bake in a moderate oven for about 1 hour. Serve with fruit juice.

CHOCOLATE SOUFFLE

2 oz. sugar	2 oz. almonds
3 eggs	½ oz. flour
1½ oz. chocolate	lemon juice or rind
pinch cinnamon	

Stiffly whisk the egg whites, add the yolks, one after another, then the flour and the peeled and chopped almonds. Add the grated chocolate, cinnamon, grated lemon rind or 1 teaspoon lemon juice and mix well together. Bake in a slow oven for 30—40 minutes. Serve with fruit juice, or custard.

TARTS

10 oz. plain flour	2 egg yolks
3 oz. sugar	lemon rind
7 oz. fat	vanilla

Sieve the dry ingredients onto a board and crumble in the fat. Make a well in the centre and break in the egg yolks. First work the dough with a knife and then with the hands. Leave in a cool place to harden. Then form into a roll, cut off small pieces and press into patty tins. The above amounts make about 40—45 tarts. Bake in a moderate oven and then turn out onto a board. When cold, fill with jam or custard. Decorate with fruit and cover with gelatine. The tarts may also be filled with whipped cream and fruit — strawberries, grapes etc. Another variation is to fill them with a nutty filling before baking and cover them with a small lattice made from strips of dough. When cooked they are glazed with a chocolate icing.

BUTTER BISCUITS

14 oz. plain flour	4 egg yolks or 2 whole eggs
9 oz. butter	vanilla
5 oz. sugar	lemon rind
	pinch cinnamon

Sieve the flour and sugar onto a board, crumble in the butter and make a well in the middle. Break in the eggs. Add the flavouring, work into a smooth dough and divide into several parts. Roll out thinly and cut into various shapes, such as stars, half-moons, rings etc., always in two sizes. Place on a greased tin and bake in a moderate oven till golden. When cold join the larger and smaller shapes together with icing or jam. Decorate the tops with icing.

SMALL BUTTER KOLACHE

Small butter kolache can be made from the tart dough on p. 188. Use a cutter to cut out small rounds from the rolled out dough. Bake half as they are and in the other half cut out a small round in the centre. Bake in a moderate oven till golden. When cold spread the full rounds with jam and cover with the rings. Sprinkle with icing sugar.

VANILLA ROLLS

1 egg yolk	5 oz. plain flour
3 oz. fat	2 oz. almonds or walnuts
1 oz. sugar	vanilla
	icing sugar for coating

Sieve the flour onto a board and add the sugar and finely ground nuts. Work the fat into the flour, using a knife. Make a well in the middle, break in the yolk and mix into a stiff dough. This must be done quickly or the fat will soften too much. Leave the dough in a cool place for a short while. Then form into a roll, cut off small picees and form these into tiny rolls. Bake in a moderate oven and while still hot roll in icing sugar flavoured with vanilla.

GINGER BISCUITS

2 eggs	8 oz. plain flour
2 egg yolks	1 teaspoon ground ginger
8 oz. sugar	pinch ammonia carbonate

Beat the eggs, yolks and sugar to a cream. Add the ground ginger and ammonia, mix well and then work in the flour. Roll out to $\frac{3}{4}$ inch thick and cut out various shapes. Place on a greased tin and leave for at least 2 hours to stand. Then bake in a moderate oven for 15—20 minutes. The biscuits are hard at first but if left in a box they soften.

BEAR'S PAWS

1 egg yolk	5 oz. nuts
9 oz. fat	2 tablespoons cocoa
12 oz. plain flour	lemon rind
8 oz. sugar	icing sugar
cinnamon	vanilla

Sieve the flour onto a board, mix in the sugar, ground nuts, cocoa, a little grated lemon rind and a pinch cinnamon. Cut in the fat and work into a dough. Press bits of dough into various small tins so that the mixture is evenly distributed and reaches up to the edge of the tin. Bake in a moderate oven. Turn out and leave to cool, then coat with icing sugar flavoured with vanilla.

LOMNICE RINGS

5 oz. fat
10 oz. flour
2 tablespoons milk
½ oz. baker's yeast

1 oz. almonds
8 oz. vanilla sugar
½ pint rum and water

Crumble the fat into the flour and add milk in which the yeast has been dissolved. Mix into a stiff dough and leave to rise. Then form into a roll, cut off equal sized pieces, roll each into a long thin roll and join up the ends to form a ring. Bake in a hot oven till golden. Then dip in water mixed with rum and coat in sugar flavoured with vanilla.

MERINGUE KISSES

5—7 oz. castor sugar to 3 egg whites

Add a few drops of water to two-thirds of the sugar and boil till it forms a thick syrup. Stiffly whisk the whites and whisk in the rest of the sugar. Continue whisking, adding the syrupy sugar a little at a time. Pipe through a plain or star-shaped nozzle onto greased paper on a greased tin so as to form little mounds. Bake in a very slow oven till very faintly pink.

GYPSY SLICES

1 egg yolk	*Filling:* 3 egg whites
2 oz. sugar	5 oz. sugar
3 oz. fat	5 oz. nuts
8 oz. flour	cinnamon
1 tablespoon milk	
lemon rind	

Sieve the flour, mix with the sugar and a little grated lemon rind and cut in the fat. Make a well in the centre and pour in the milk with the egg yolk. Work into a dough and roll out. Beat the 3 egg whites with the sugar and add the ground nuts and a pinch of cinnamon. Spread the filling onto the dough and cut into slices with a wetted knife. Bake on a greased tin in a hot oven.

SCALES

1 egg	1 gill milk
3 oz. fat	1 teaspoon salt
8 oz. plain flour	1 teaspoon caraway seeds

Sieve the flour and salt onto a board. Crumble in the fat and mix with milk to an elastic dough. Roll out as thin as paper and carefully transter to a greased tin. When it is in the tin cut it into small squares. Brush with egg and bake in a moderate oven until golden.

CHOCOLATE CAKE

5 eggs	2 tablespoons cocoa
7 oz. sugar	*Filling:* $\frac{3}{4}$ pint milk
3 oz. nuts	1 tablespoon fine
3 oz. flour	semolina
$\frac{1}{2}$ teaspoon baking powder	3 oz. butter
	3 oz. sugar
	rum essence

Whisk 6 tablespoons hot water and egg yolks together for about 5 minutes. Add the sugar and continue whisking. Then add the ground nuts, flour, baking powder, cocoa and stiffly whisked egg whites. Grease a cake tin, sprinkle with flour and pile in the dough. Bake in a moderate oven till golden. For the cream filling boil the fine semolina with the milk to make a thick pudding. Cool. Now cream the butter and sugar separately and then add the pudding. Finally add a little rum essence. Cut the cake in half when cold, fill with the creamy filling and decorate.

MERINGUE CAKE

5 egg whites	5 oz. icing sugar
7 oz. castor sugar	vanilla essence

Stiffly whisk the egg whites, beat in the castor sugar and a few drops of vanilla essence and fold in the icing sugar. Draw rings on greased paper and onto these pipe the meringue mixture as illustrated opposite, making one plain round and one fancy ring. Sprinkle lightly with sugar and dry out in a slow oven. Carefully turn onto a board, upside down, and peel off the paper. When quite cold fill with chocolate butter cream or whipped cream.

MERINGUE CAKE WITH CREAM

9 egg whites   1 oz. flour
4 oz. sugar   vanilla essence
4 oz. walnuts or almonds   whipped cream

Grind the walnuts or almonds, and mix with the 3 egg whites. Add the sugar, a little vanilla essence and beat well. Stiffly whisk the rest of the whites and add together with the flour to the nuts. Pipe 12 small meringues onto a tin for decorating the cake, sprinkle with sugar and bake in a slow oven till slightly coloured. Bake the rest of the mixture in two cake tins, join with whipped cream and decorate with the small meringues.

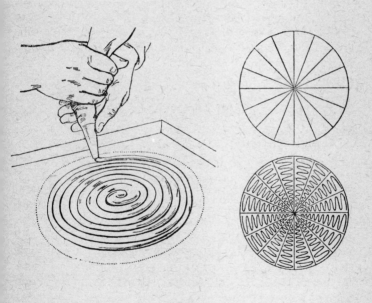

TWO-COLOURED LAYER CAKE

Layer 1:	Layer 2:	Cream:
5 eggs	5 eggs	1 egg yolk
5 oz. sugar	6 oz. sugar	5 oz. butter
1 oz. crumbled sponge	4 oz. flour	4 oz. sugar
1 oz. chopped nuts		
1 oz. chocolate		
3 oz. flour		

Layer 1: Beat the egg yolks and sugar to a thick cream. Add the softened chocolate or cocoa, warmed with a small piece of butter, and beat for a few more minutes. Stiffly whisk the egg whites and mix with the nuts, crumbled sponge and flour. Add to the yolks and bake in a moderate oven in a cake tin. When cold cut in half.

Layer 2: Stiffly whisk the egg whites, fold in the sugar, egg yolks and flour. Place on a baking tin to form a layer about ½ inch thick and bake in a hot oven to prevent the edges drying out.

Cream: Cream the sugar, butter, and egg yolk.

Spread a little cream on layer 2 and cut it into strips about 1 inch wide. Spread some cream on the bottom half of layer 1 and place the strips from layer 2 spirally on it, starting from the centre, until the whole of layer 1 has been covered. Spread with some more cream and cover with the second half of layer 1. Decorate the top with a white or cocoa icing. If it is to be decorated with cream twice the amount of cream filling must be made. The spirals may also be made as follows. Roll up the second layer while still hot; when cool unroll, spread with cream and again roll up. Cut into slices about 1 inch thick. The slices must be the same thickness or the cake will look crooked. Place them close together on top of the first layer, cut side downwards, cover with cream and then add the top half of layer 1.

HONEY WAFER CAKE

8 oz. plain flour
1 egg
3 oz. sugar
1 oz. fat
1 teaspoon bicarbonate of soda
1 tablespoon honey
little vanilla essence

chopped nuts or chocolate to
decorate
Filling: 1 pint milk
3 oz. sugar
1 tablespoon cocoa
2 oz. butter
1 oz. cornflour

Whisk the honey, sugar, egg, vanilla, and fat to a thick cream over a saucepan of boiling water. Add the soda and after whisking for a little while longer remove from the stove and fold in the flour. When cool turn onto a floured board. Divide into five parts and roll out each to wafer thinness. Bake in a moderate oven in a greased tin. When golden remove from the oven and use a knife to take from the tin while still warm. Mix a little of the milk for the cream filling with the cornflour. Bring the rest of the milk and the sugar to the boil, add the cornflour and stir. Boil for a few minutes, then remove from the stove. When cold add the butter and cocoa. Join the wafers with the cream filling, cover with a weight and leave for several hours in a cool place. Then decorate with the remaining cream, sprinkle the sides and top with roasted chopped nuts or grated chocolate.

HONEY CAKE

3 eggs   cinnamon
5 oz. honey or syrup   cloves
6 oz. flour   vanilla essence
2 oz. nuts   lemon rind
1 oz. sugar

Stiffly whisk the egg whites and the melted honey, a few drops
at a time. Whisk the egg yolks with the sugar to a cream and
add to the whites. Season with pinch cinnamon, cloves,
a little vanilla essence and lemon rind. Thicken with ground
nuts and flour. Pile into a greased cake tin and bake in a very
moderate oven for about 30 minutes. When cold cover with
a rum icing (see p. 181).

ICED CAKE

5—6 egg yolks   8 oz. ground almonds
7 oz. butter   ½ pint milk
8 oz. sugar   vanilla essence
½ pint whipped cream   3 oz. sponge fingers

Cream the butter and sugar and gradually add the egg yolks.
Then sprinkle in the ground almonds and add the milk with
vanilla essence, a few drops at a time. The mixture must be
beaten for a long time. Fill a cake tin with alternate layers of
sponge fingers and cream, ending with a layer of sponge
fingers. Place in a refrigerator or on ice and when cold turn
out and decorate with whipped cream.

CHOCOLATE RIBBED LOAF

6 eggs	pinch cinnamon
5 oz. sugar	1 bread roll
3 oz. chocolate	a little wine
5 oz. almonds	jam
	1 oz. almonds for decorating

Beat the egg yolks and sugar till creamy. Add the melted chocolate or cocoa heated with a little fat and sugar, and the crumbled bread roll which has been soaked in a little wine. Chop the almonds and add to the mixture together with the stiffly whisked egg whites.

Three-quarters fill a greased and floured mould and bake in a slowish oven for 30—40 minutes. Leave to stand for a while and then turn out. When cold, spread with a thin layer of jam and cover with chocolate or cocoa icing (see Indianky, p. 162). Decorate with split almonds.

COFFEE CREAM

½ pint milk	3 oz. sugar
2 egg yolks	about 25 sponge fingers
1 teaspoon vanilla sugar	½ pint whipped cream
3 tablespoons strong black coffee	pinch flour
3 oz. butter	

Beat the egg yolks into the milk, add a pinch of flour, a little sugar flavoured with vanilla and the strong black coffee. Bring slowly to the boil and stir all the time. When it thickens remove from the stove. Cream the butter with the sugar and mix in the coffee cream, a spoonful at a time. Place alternate layers of sponge fingers and cream in small bowls. Leave in a cool place overnight and then decorate with whipped cream.

COTTAGE CHEESE CREAM

1 lb. cottage cheese	3 eggs
3 oz. butter	3 tablespoons rum
½ pint whipped cream	8 oz. fruit
vanilla essence	5 oz. sugar

Sieve the soft cottage cheese and add the butter, sugar, a little vanilla essence, 3 tablespoons whipped cream and the rum and whisk well together. Then add the egg yolks and stiffly whisked egg whites. Pile the cream and fruit into a bowl and decorate with whipped cream.

PINEAPPLE CREAM

1 pint milk	1 oz. gelatine
3 egg yolks	2 tablespoons rum
3 oz. sugar with vanilla	about 25 sponge fingers
1 pint whipped cream	piquant jam
	pineapple

Beat together the milk, egg yolks and sugar flavoured with vanilla, place on the stove and whisk until it thickens. Then add the gelatine, dissolved in 2 tablespoons hot water and 2 tablespoons rum. Mix well together and leave to cool. Spread jam on the sponge fingers and press together. Place a layer of sponge fingers in a glass bowl and pour over the cream. Leave in a cool place to set and then decorate with whipped cream and alternating layers of sponge fingers with cream and pineapple.

INDEX OF RECIPES

Printed in Czechoslovakia